CULTURES OF THE WORLD

LITHUANIA

Sakina Kagda

MARSHALL CAVENDISH

New York • London • Sydney

Reference edition published 1997 by
Marshall Cavendish Corporation
99 White Plains Road
Tarrytown
New York 10591

© Times Editions Pte Ltd 1997

Originated and designed by
Times Books International, an imprint of
Times Editions Pte Ltd

Printed in Singapore

Library of Congress Cataloging-in-Publication Data:
Kagda, Sakina.
    Lithuania / Sakina Kagda.
        p. cm.—(Cultures of the World)
    Includes bibliographical references (p.) and index.
    Summary: Examines the geography, history, government,
economy, and culture of this newly independent Baltic state.
    ISBN 0-7614-0681-6 (lib. bdg.)
    1. Lithuania—Juvenile literature. [1. Lithuania.]
I. Title. II. Series.
DK505.23.K34   1997
947.93—dc21   96–29460
                    CIP
                    AC

INTRODUCTION

 LOCATED IN THE EXACT geographical center of Europe, Lithuania was once one of the largest and most powerful countries in Europe. However, the power of the Grand Duchy was progressively depleted by its union with Poland and by the assaults of Germany, Sweden, and Russia. It enjoyed a golden age of independence between the World Wars, only to come under the crushing control of Germany and the Soviet Union.

Since achieving independence in 1991, Lithuania is entering a new era. This is a time of great optimism as well as new fears. Lithuanians are an open and confident people with a rich culture of rural traditions, pre-Christian and Catholic religious practices, and a strong nationalistic spirit. They see their country as the natural leader of the Baltic states. This volume of *Cultures of the World* examines a complex nation that is striving to forge a role in the new Europe.

CONTENTS

A dramatic sculpture of the three muses rises above the entrance to the Academic Drama Theater in Vilnius.

CONTENTS

Art and music combine on
a city street.

GEOGRAPHY

LITHUANIA IS AT THE HEART of Europe. The exact geographical center of Europe, certified in 1989 by the French National Geography Institute, is located 17 miles (27 km) north of the capital, Vilnius. Lithuania's neighbors are Latvia in the north, Belarus in the east and south, and Poland and the Kaliningrad region of the Russian Federation in the southwest. On the west it borders the Baltic Sea.

Lithuania covers 25,174 square miles (65,201 square km), a little more than West Virginia. It is the largest of the three former Soviet republics bordering the Baltic Sea—Lithuania, Latvia, and Estonia. These three are often referred to as the Baltic states. They share a similar topography as well as many common cultural elements.

Opposite: **The Nemunas River winds through fertile farmlands and forests.**

Below: **Light snow covers the ground in Klaipeda, on the Baltic Sea coast.**

7

PHYSICAL GEOGRAPHY

The Baltic states are characterized by flat farmlands alternating with low, rolling hills formed during the last Ice Age. Many small rivers and lakes, interspersed with pine forests, give character to the landscape. The plains sometimes sink into large tracts of swampland. The region is dotted with ancient city centers surrounded by Soviet-era concrete housing blocks.

Lithuania can be roughly divided into eight regions:

- **AUKSTAITIJA** ("highland" in Lithuanian) in the east is characterized by gently rolling hills, pine forests, and hundreds of lakes.
- **ZEMAITIJA** is a moderately high area in the northwest and is traditionally noted for its dialect, roadside shrines, and local dress.
- **THE CENTRAL LOWLANDS** cover northern Lithuania between Aukstaitija and Zemaitija. This flat land is largely agricultural, although the cities of Siauliai, Joniskis, and Panevezys are heavily industrialized.
- **DZUKIJA** is a hilly southern region east of the Nemunas River.

- **SUVALKIJA** is in the south to the west of the Nemunas.
- **THE COAST** is marked by sandy beaches and magnificent dunes.
- **THE KAUNAS REGION** is generally flat and agricultural except for the steep hills bordering the Nemunas River valley.
- **THE VILNIUS REGION** is a hilly area with many farms as well as the capital and its surrounding multicultural district. Lithuania's highest point, a 963 feet (294 m) hill called Juozapines, is located in this area.

Snow piles up along the Baltic shoreline during Lithuania's long, cold winters.

CLIMATE

The climate in Lithuania is transitional between maritime and continental. In the coastal zone, the climate is maritime. In the eastern part of the country, it is continental. The mean annual temperature is about 43°F (6°C) with a mean temperature in July of 63°F (17°C). There are four distinct seasons. Summers have moderate heat, adequate humidity, and a sufficient number of bright days for vegetation growth. Fall and winter are cold and long.

The mean annual rainfall varies from 21 inches (53 cm) in the central lowlands to 37 inches (93 cm) on the southwestern slopes of the Zemaitija hills. The greatest amount of rain falls in August at the seaside. The growing season is relatively short, varying between 169 and 202 days.

"Where the Sesupe
and Nemunas
rivers flow/
There is our
country, lovely
Lithuania."

—Maironis,
a Lithuanian poet

RIVERS, LAKES, AND WOODLANDS

Lithuania is a land of outstanding scenic beauty, with meandering rivers, thousands of lakes, and ancient woodlands rich in wildlife. Forests, including pine, spruce, birch, black alder, aspen, oak, and ash, cover 28 percent of the total land area. Large tracts of land are also covered with bogs and marsh.

Lithuania has a large, dense river network. The waters of the Minija, Musa, Venta, Jura, Sesupe, Dubysa, and Nemunas rivers flow through the country. There are 722 rivers of six miles (10 km) and longer, most of them tributaries of the Nemunas, which flows for 582 miles (937 km). Lithuanians like to refer to their country as Nemunasland, due to the great love they have for the Nemunas. In pre-Christian times, waters and forests were considered to be sacred.

Forests were considered sacred in the ancient Lithuanian religion, and Lithuanians today retain a strong respect for nature.

There are over 4,000 lakes in Lithuania, 25 of them with an area of more than 386 square miles (1,000 square km). The largest freshwater lake is Kauno Marios ("Kaunas Sea"), a dam east of Kaunas, with an area of 2,451 square miles (6,350 square km). The dam has turned this part of the Nemunas River into a recreational area, and pleasure-boats are still able to make the journey from Kaunas to the Baltic Sea. The deepest, Lake Tauragnai, is 200 feet (61 m) deep. Most lakes are concentrated in the Aukstaitija hills around Ignalina.

11

The marshes of Zuvintas natural reserve in Suval-kija region support more than 600 species of plants and 250 species of birds. Zuvintas is one of four natural reserves, which are smaller than national parks.

NATIONAL PARKS

The Soviet years contributed to the preservation of nature in Lithuania largely because of mismanagement of the country. The percentage of unused land increased after 1940 as the rural population migrated to other countries or was deported to Siberia. As farmlands decreased, forests took over the abandoned land. Lithuania retains large tracts of beaches, woodlands, and wilderness that have disappeared elsewhere in Europe because of overdevelopment.

Lithuania has vast reserves of wilderness protected by its five national parks. The first national park, the Aukstaitija National Park, was designated in 1974 and covers an area of 74,130 acres (30,000 hectares). Over 70 percent of this park is pine forest. The park's beautiful lakes and rivers attract tourists, naturalists, and ethnographers.

Dzukija National Park was established to protect the old villages, historical and cultural monuments, and forests of southeastern Lithuania. Eighty-five percent of the park is covered by woods.

On the Baltic coast is Kursiu Marios, Lithuania's largest inland body of water. A narrow strip of land called Kursiu Nerija (also known as the Courland Spit) separates Kursiu Marios from the Baltic Sea. Kursiu Nerija National Park is located on this spit. Until the 15th century the spit was covered with forest, but as a result of heavy logging the sand cover was nearly destroyed, and shifting sand dunes sometimes covered whole villages. There is now an attempt to reforest the area to stabilize the dunes.

The other national parks are at Trakai and Zemaitija.

A WILDLIFE PARADISE

Because of its large areas of forest and marsh, Lithuania has become a preferred home for a variety of animals and birds. Ducks, waders, terns, and swans can be found in the coastal wetlands, while birds of prey, corncrakes, and white storks inhabit the uplands and hooded crows haunt the cities. The forests and rivers are home to elk, deer, martyns, lynx, boars, beavers, and otters. Occasionally one can even find brown bears.

Trophy hunting is now becoming popular with European visitors, such as Germans who go to Lithuania to hunt wolves. This brings Lithuania some much-needed foreign money. Wild game caught by professional hunters has always been a popular item on Lithuanian menus, but recreational hunting is not a common pastime in the Baltic states.

Lithuanians love flowers and will give them for any occasion. Beautiful wild-flowers and gardens can be seen growing all over the country.

Vilnius is situated in a picturesque valley where the fast-flowing Neris River meets the Vilnia River.

CITIES

Lithuania's largest cities are Vilnius (population 591,000), Kaunas (430,000), Klaipeda (206,000), Siauliai (148,000), and Panevezys (129,000).

VILNIUS Lithuania's capital, Vilnius, is one of the major industrial, scientific, and cultural centers of the Baltic region. The city was founded in 1323 by Grand Duke Gediminas. After dreaming of an ironclad wolf howling from a hill near the Vilnia River, he invited merchants and craftsmen to settle on the site and build a city. By the 16th century, Vilnius had became one of the major cities of Europe. Vilnius University, founded in 1579, is one of the oldest institutions of higher learning in Europe.

The numerous churches that characterize Vilnius were converted to other uses during the Soviet years, but are now being restored. The city's first church, the cathedral, was built in 1387. Rebuilt repeatedly over the centuries, it was the first church to be reconstructed following independence.

KAUNAS Kaunas is Lithuania's second largest city. Its rivalry with Vilnius dates to 1920, when it became the provisional capital after Vilnius was occupied by Poland. Today it is the major commercial center of the country. Kaunas is the most Lithuanian of all Lithuanian cities. Eighty-seven percent of its population are ethnic Lithuanians, and much of the old city has survived both World War II and the Soviet period.

TRAKAI

Trakai was the capital of the Grand Duchy during the Middle Ages. Today it is a popular resort village in a beautiful region of lakes, forests, and hills west of Vilnius. The center of Trakai is its castle, probably built by Grand Duke Jaunutis (Gediminas' son) between 1362 and 1382. The complex of defensive fortifications and castle stands on a peninsula and an island. It is the only island castle still standing in northeastern Europe. The castle is now impressively restored and stands as a monument to the past glory of the medieval Lithuanian state.

The town of Trakai consists of old wooden buildings along with a few modern ones. It is the home of the Karaites, a tribe of Turks brought to Lithuania in the late 14th century by Grand Duke Vytautas to serve as his bodyguards.

HISTORY

LITHUANIA HAS HAD A SHORT HISTORY as an independent nation, but a very long one as a separate culture. Today, as Lithuanians struggle to establish their young country economically and politically, they look back for inspiration to the time when the Grand Duchy of Lithuania was one of the largest countries in Europe, stretching from the Baltic Sea in the north to the Black Sea in the south, and from Poland in the west nearly to Moscow in the east. More recently, they can look back on the tranquil period earlier this century when Lithuania was an independent and successful nation.

These periods of greatness have, however, been overshadowed in Lithuania's history by centuries of domination by its powerful neighbors—Poland, Russia, Germany, and Sweden, all of whom have vied for control of this strategically important territory. During these long periods of domination, Lithuanians have struggled to maintain their separate identity and culture. Through the years, they have preserved their language, their religion, and their traditions in spite of continued attempts to obliterate all traces of ancient Lithuania.

Above: **Gediminas Tower, the oldest settlement of Vilnius, was built by Grand Duke Gediminas in the 14th century.**

Opposite: **A memorial to the civilians who were killed by Soviet troops in 1991 stands outside Lithuania's parliament.**

THE HOUSE OF LIUTAURUS

Most of the grand dukes of Lithuania belonged to a single dynasty. These grand dukes and their reigns were: Vytenis (1295–1316), Gediminas (1316–41), Jaunutis (1341–45), Algirdas and Kestutis (1345–77), Jogaila (1377–92), Vytautas the Great (1392–1430), Svitrigaila (1430–32), Sigismund (1432–40), Casimir (1440–92), and Alexander (1492–1506).

*Baltic tribes of the
9th–12th centuries:*
Lithuanians
Curonians
Semigallians
Selonians
Samogitians
Nadruvians
Prussians
Jotvings
Skalvians
Latgalians

THE EARLY LITHUANIANS

The prehistoric inhabitants of the Baltic region were nomadic hunters and, at a later date, farmers. In around 2,500 B.C., Indo-European tribes spread across the region that is now western Russia, Ukraine, Belarus, and Poland, eventually becoming concentrated along the Baltic shoreline. They merged with the indigenous population and formed a number of distinct tribes in the territory that is now Lithuania. At the end of the first century A.D., the Roman historian Tacitus described the people living around the Baltic Sea in his history of Germany. He mentioned that they traded in amber and that they were able farmers, saying that in the growing of corn and other crops they worked "with more patience than is customary among the lazy Germans."

THE VYTIS

The state emblem of the Republic of Lithuania is the *vytis* ("VEE-tis"), the White Knight. It is a white knight in armor on a white horse, holding a raised sword in his right hand. A blue shield on the left shoulder of the knight has a double gold cross.

The charging knight was first used as the state emblem in 1366 on the seal of Grand Duke Algirdas. With minor stylistic changes, the vytis remained the state emblem of the Grand Duchy of Lithuania until the 18th century. When Lithuania was annexed by the Russian Empire in 1795, the vytis was incorporated into the imperial state emblem.

In time, the charging knight came to be understood as a riding knight chasing an intruder out of his country. Banned under Soviet rule, the vytis became a symbol of the Lithuanian drive for independence.

In its heyday in the 15th century, the Grand Duchy of Lithuania was the most powerful state in central Europe.

From the 2nd to the 5th century A.D., the Baltic tribes enjoyed a golden age in which they developed a trading empire that covered northeastern Europe. During the 9th and 10th centuries, Vikings from Scandinavia launched attacks on the prosperous coastal regions of the Baltic, and the Baltic tribes and the Vikings alternately fought and traded with each other.

The 10th century also saw the start of feudalism in the Baltic region and the emergence of the Lithuanians—the largest tribe—as dominant on Lithuanian territory. Protected by impenetrable forests and thousands of lakes, Lithuania remained isolated up until the 14th century.

THE GRAND DUCHY

During the 13th century, German crusaders invaded the Baltic region in a bid to conquer and Christianize the last pagan tribes in Europe. The Knights of the Sword and their successors, the Teutonic Knights, conquered the tribes of Latvia and Estonia, creating the country of Livonia.

As the other Baltic tribes fell to the German knights, only the Lithuanians succeeded in maintaining their independence. In 1236, Mindaugas united the small feudal states of Lithuania into a duchy. The united Lithuania struck a powerful blow against the Knights of the Sword at Siauliai. In 1251 Mindaugas adopted the Catholic faith in order to be crowned king by Pope Innocent. However, in the face of continued problems with the crusaders, he abandoned Christianity and sacrificed a Christian princess to the god Perkunas. Mindaugas was assassinated in 1263.

The formation of the state was completed by the grand dukes Traidenis (who reigned 1270–82) and Vytenis (1295–1316). Vytenis left a large state with clearly defined policies to his brother Gediminas (1316–41). Under Gediminas, the Lithuanian territory was extended as far as Kiev and the Black Sea.

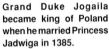

Grand Duke Jogaila became king of Poland when he married Princess Jadwiga in 1385.

ALLIANCE WITH POLAND

The Lithuanian leaders were successful in resisting the continued attacks by the Teutonic Knights, but under increased pressure in the late 14th century, they decided to ally themselves with Poland, which was also fighting the crusaders. In 1385 Lithuanian nobles arranged the marriage of Grand Duke Jogaila of Lithuania to 13-year-old Princess Jadwiga of Poland. The match was quite desirable—Jadwiga's husband would become King of Poland—but there were conditions attached: Jogaila must become a Christian and convert his whole empire as well. Jogaila was baptized as Ladislaus and assumed the crowns of Poland and Lithuania. Lithuania was the last European country to adopt Christianity.

After the marriage of Jogaila and Jadwiga, Polish feudal lords tried to abolish the Grand Duchy of Lithuania, but their efforts were resisted by the Lithuanian aristocracy and Lithuania maintained its separate identity. Jogaila's reign in Poland (1386–1434) started a long period of the Lithuanian-Polish common history which lasted until the 18th century.

VYTAUTAS THE GREAT

The position of grand duke of Lithuania was given to Jogaila's cousin Vytautas, who became the last of the great Lithuanian rulers. He drove back the Turks, and under his rule, from 1392 to 1430, the Grand Duchy became one of the largest states in Europe.

The Teutonic Knights continued their attempts to conquer Lithuania. The Lithuanians and the Poles defeated them at the Battle of Tannenberg in 1410, ending the Knights' ambitions in the Baltic.

Poland put its cultural stamp on Lithuania. The Lithuanian nobility were quick to appreciate that they would gain personally from Poland's rigid and efficient social and political order. The pre-Christian religion vanished and Roman Catholicism flourished. The nobility spoke Latin at court and Polish elsewhere.

Weakened by increasing fights with Russia, in 1569 Lithuania joined with Poland to form the Union of Lublin, "a commonwealth of two nations." Lithuania retained its territory, legislation, treasury, and army, but shared Poland's king and government. The Grand Duchy slowly declined.

The Grand Duchy of Lithuania reached its greatest extent during the reign of Vytautas the Great.

A Russian Orthodox church in the Aukstaitija region.

RUSSIAN OCCUPATION

The disintegration of the Grand Duchy in the 18th century led to an economic, social, and political crisis exacerbated by wars with Sweden, Russia, and Turkey. Lithuania was partitioned three times (in 1772, 1793, 1795). In 1795, Lithuania was absorbed by Russia, except for a small part that was incorporated into Prussia.

In reaction to peasant uprisings, Russia began an intensive process of Russification. The goal was to eradicate all traces of ancient Lithuania. Landholding rights were limited to followers of the Russian Orthodox religion. Vilnius University was closed in 1832, and only Russians were admitted to schools above the elementary level. The Lithuanian language and the Latin alphabet in which it was written were banned.

Lithuanians resisted the Russian occupation. An uprising in 1832 failed. In its wake, Russification became more intense, but resistance continued. Lithuanian books were printed in Prussian Lithuania and secretly brought to Lithuania. From 1891 to 1893, 37,718 Lithuanian books and newspapers were confiscated by the Russian border police. From 1900 to 1902, the figure was 56,182. In 1883, the first Lithuanian newspaper, *Ausra*, was published. When that was brutally suppressed, *Varpas* appeared. The ban on the press was lifted in 1904.

PROCLAMATION OF AN INDEPENDENT STATE

Antanas Smetona, the first president of independent Lithuania.

Demands for Lithuanian autonomy continued to surface. However, World War I turned Lithuania into a battlefield; in the fall of 1915, the whole of its territory was occupied by the Germans. On February 16, 1918, Lithuania proclaimed its independence. Germany recognized the new state in 1918, Russia in 1920, and in 1921 it was admitted to the League of Nations. Relations with the Vatican were settled in 1927.

Lithuania continued to have problems with its neighbors. In October 1920, Poland occupied Vilnius. The capital had to be transferred to Kaunas.

A democratic constitution was adopted in 1922, and the litas became the currency. Antanas Smetona was elected Lithuania's first president. He was president from 1918 to 1920, and then again from 1926 to 1940, after an interim of unstable governments.

During these 22 years of independence, Lithuania's economy grew to compete with those of Western European countries. This is a time that Lithuanians look back on with nostalgia, and they have longed to return to it through the 50 long years that followed as a Soviet republic.

Flowers and candles are laid along the railway tracks in memory of the 200,000 Lithuanians who were deported to Soviet labor camps.

SOVIET AND GERMAN OCCUPATIONS

On June 14, 1940, the Soviet Union issued an ultimatum to Lithuania demanding that Lithuania's government resign. On the night of July 11, 1940, more than 2,000 people were deported, and in a few days Lithuania was incorporated into the Soviet Union. Many countries never recognized this incorporation.

The Russian occupation was interrupted by the German army, which occupied Lithuania from 1941 until 1944. During this time, the Nazis sent 160,000 Lithuanians to their deaths in concentration camps, including more than 130,000 Lithuanian Jews. The large Jewish community in Vilnius was almost entirely wiped out.

In 1944, the Soviet Union once again brought Lithuania under its communist regime. There were mass deportations, in which the Soviet government sent some 200,000 Lithuanians to labor camps in Siberia. Many of those deported died along the way. Farms were reorganized in the collective farm program and the Lithuanian economy became subordinated to the needs of the greater Soviet economy. Religion was suppressed, as were other aspects of Lithuanian culture. Many freedoms were eliminated.

By the late 1980s, the Soviet economy was in dire straits. The Soviet leader, Mikhail Gorbachev, introduced the reform policies of glasnost (openness) and perestroika (restructuring). Under these new policies, Soviet citizens were encouraged to voice their opinions and to participate in the reform of the Soviet system. This new openness led to the emergence of independence movements in many of the Soviet republics. One of these was Lithuania.

RE-ESTABLISHMENT OF INDEPENDENCE

On February 7, 1990, the Lithuanian Communist Party declared the 1945 Soviet annexation illegal. They were joined by Sajudis, a pro-independence party. In national elections held in 1990, Sajudis won a majority in the parliament. By the Act of March 11, 1990, the Lithuanian parliament declared the restoration of the independence of the Republic of Lithuania. Vytautas Landsbergis, the new leader of parliament, formed a cabinet of ministers under Prime Minister Kazimiera Prunskiene, and adopted a constitution. The Soviet government declared an economic embargo and sent tanks to Vilnius, but in the face of international disapproval, they agreed to negotiate.

Little progress was made in the negotiations, and on January 13, 1991, Soviet tanks occupied radio and television stations. Fourteen Lithuanians were killed in the confrontation. In Moscow an attempted coup failed, and on September 6, 1991, Lithuania again declared the independent Republic of Lithuania. This time the resolution was accepted. Lithuania was admitted to the United Nations in September 1991.

The coffins of the civilians who were killed by Soviet troops in 1991 are decked with Lithuanian flags. These people are remembered in Lithuania as martyrs for their country.

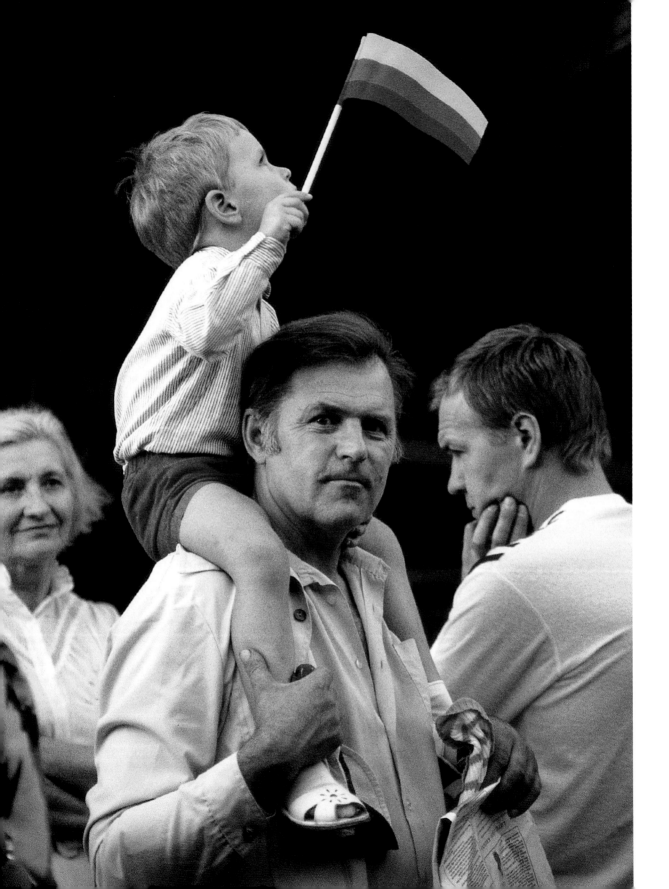

GOVERNMENT

THE LITHUANIAN STATE is an independent democratic republic. The foundations of the political and social system are stipulated in the constitution of the Republic of Lithuania, which was adopted in October 1992. It establishes the rights, freedoms, and obligations of citizens. The constitution states that state power in Lithuania is "exercised by the Seimas [parliament], the President, the Government, and the Judiciary."

Opposite: **Waving the Lithuanian flag in Vilnius.**

Left: **A political rally organized by a Lithuanian workers' union.**

Voting in Lithuania's first democratic election in 1990.

THE CONSTITUTION

On May 18, 1989, the Lithuanian Supreme Soviet adopted a declaration of Lithuanian sovereignty that asserted the supremacy of Lithuania's laws over Soviet legislation. A general election in February and March 1990 resulted in a pro-independence majority in the Supreme Soviet, and that body declared the restoration of Lithuanian independence. The Supreme Soviet was renamed the Supreme Council. It restored the pre-1940 name of the country (the Republic of Lithuania) and adopted the Provisional Fundamental Law of the Republic of Lithuania, which restored portions of the Lithuanian constitution of 1938. It established the rights, freedoms, and duties of the country's citizens.

A new constitution was approved in a national referendum in October 1992. It created a strong presidential system with a legislature of 141 elected representatives and a Council of Ministers headed by a prime minister.

THE SEIMAS

The highest state authority is the Seimas ("SAY-i-mahs"), formerly called the Supreme Council, which is directly elected by universal adult suffrage. The Seimas elects a head of state, the president, for a maximum of two consecutive five-year terms. The Seimas also appoints the government in the form of a Council of Ministers, which is the highest authority of executive power. The Council of Ministers is headed by the prime minister. Supreme judicial authority is vested in the Procurator-General of the Republic of Lithuania, who is also appointed by the Seimas.

The Seimas in session.

As the highest state authority, the Seimas has the power to adopt laws, consider drafts on the program produced by the government, approve the budget of the government, establish the state institutions provided by the law, appoint and dismiss heads of state institutions, and settle other issues pertaining to state power.

During the elections that took place on October 25, 1992, 141 deputies were elected to the Seimas of the Republic of Lithuania. Deputies have a term of office of four years. They must be at least 25 years old with a permanent residence in Lithuania.

The chairman of the Seimas or his deputy presides over Seimas meetings. In 1992 Ceslovas Jursenas was elected as chairman of the Seimas. The Seimas structure and questions of procedure are determined by the Seimas Statute. The Seimas headquarters is in Vilnius.

THE PRESIDENT

The president of the Republic of Lithuania is the highest official of the state. He or she represents the country and is elected by citizens of Lithuania for a term of five years on the basis of universal suffrage by secret ballot. The president acts in conformity with the constitution and other laws and:

- resolves major issues of foreign policy and conducts foreign policy jointly with the government
- signs international treaties of the Republic of Lithuania, submitting them to the Seimas for ratification
- with Seimas approval, appoints the prime minister and empowers him or her to form the government (Council of Ministers), and confirms its composition

Lithuanian soldiers on parade. Lithuania did not have an army during the Soviet era.

- appoints and discharges state officials
- submits candidates for the supreme court and the constitutional court for the consideration of the Seimas
- with Seimas approval, appoints and discharges the chiefs of the armed forces and security service
- confers the highest military titles
- proclaims a state of emergency as provided by law
- makes annual reports at the Seimas on the current situation in Lithuania as well as its domestic and foreign policy
- announces elections
- signs and announces the laws passed by the Seimas, or hands them over to the Seimas for reconsideration
- performs other powers provided by the constitution
- exercises his or her power by issuing acts and decrees

ALGIRDAS BRAZAUSKAS

The Sajudis (Lithuanian Reform) movement won a majority in parliament in 1990, but a year later, as winter set in, many Lithuanians still had no heating or hot water. The voters became unhappy about unemployment, high prices, and fuel shortages, and when elections were held in October and November 1992, the pro-independence Lithuanian Democratic Labor Party (LDLP), formerly the Communist Party, was returned to power.

Algirdas Mykolas Brazauskas (*pictured right*) was elected president of Lithuania during the first direct presidential elections in February 1993. He was a member of the LDLP but has subsequently resigned from the party.

Vytautas Landsbergis was leader of the Sajudis movement when it gained a majority of parliament in March 1990. He became the first leader of Lithuania after independence.

THE GOVERNMENT

The government of Lithuania is composed of the prime minister and 16 ministers. The prime minister is appointed or dismissed by the president with the approval of the Seimas. Ministers are appointed and dismissed by the president upon the recommendation of the prime minister.

The government controls affairs of the country, ensures state and civilian security, and carries out laws, resolutions of the Seimas on the enforcement of laws, and decrees of the president. It also enters into and maintains diplomatic relations with foreign countries and international organizations and performs the duties specified in the constitution and other laws.

Since coming to power, the government has faced a twofold challenge. It has had to establish the legal, institutional, and regulatory framework of an independent democratic state. At the same time, it has had to restructure the centralized economy into a free market economy while reducing economic dependence on the former Soviet Union.

THE JUDICIAL SYSTEM

The judicial system consists of a constitutional court, a supreme court, a court of appeals, and district and local courts. The constitutional court consists of nine judges appointed for nonrenewable terms of nine years. It determines whether laws enacted by the Seimas or actions of the president or Council of Ministers are in conformity with the constitution.

The Seimas appoints the judges of the constitutional court and the supreme court. Judges of the court of appeals are appointed by the president with approval from the Seimas. Judges of district and local courts are appointed by the president. Public prosecutors conduct criminal cases on behalf of the state.

CORRUPTION AND CRIME

Lithuanian government is not without its problems. Politics still bears a strong resemblance to that of the Soviet era, and many Lithuanians are becoming disillusioned. Only 45 percent of eligible voters participated in local elections in 1995. Few legal constraints govern politicians' business interests, and there is widespread concern over political corruption.

The judiciary and the police are staffed with people who were trained during the Soviet era, and corruption is increasingly common. The result is a wave of organized crime, burglary, and car theft. Street crime is also on the rise.

This police officer in Kaunas is wearing the new uniform of the Lithuanian police force.

ECONOMY

SINCE INDEPENDENCE in September 1991, Lithuania has made steady progress in developing a market economy. To ensure economic stability after the breakup of the Soviet Union, Lithuania and the other two Baltic states, Latvia and Estonia, launched a program of land reform and market-oriented economic reforms in November 1991. The latter cover price structure, government spending, foreign trade, banking and monetary policy, competition, taxes, ownership, and privatization laws. Over 40 percent of state property has been privatized, and trade is diversifying, with a gradual shift away from the former Soviet Union to international markets. During the Soviet occupation, 5 percent of exports were sent to the West; now the figure is nearer to 45 percent.

Lithuania's economic profile shows a strong bias toward agriculture. Principal exports are electricity, light industrial products such as textiles, and food products. Principal imports include petroleum and natural gas, machinery, chemicals, and light industrial products.

Lithuania has a skilled workforce with expertise in modern technology developed during the years when the Baltic states were used as an economic and industrial laboratory by the Soviet Union. The country is superbly positioned for international trade as it has access to major adjoining markets. To its east in Russia lies the largest emerging consumer group of today and to its west is one of the world's most prosperous regions.

Above: **Klaipeda is the center of the fishing industry.**

Opposite: **Lithuania has more farming machinery than Latvia or Estonia, but the machinery is old, and it is still common to see horses, carts, and scythes.**

THE SEARCH FOR ENERGY

Lithuania produces a great deal of electrical power through a hydroelectricity station near Vilnius and a nuclear power plant near Ignalina. An oil refinery in Mazeikiai receives crude oil from Russia and exports refined products through the port at Klaipeda. Lithuania produces twice as much power as it uses and exports electricity to Latvia and Belarus.

However, the country is severely lacking in fuel resources. Although peat deposits supply some of the country's energy needs, other fuel supplies are imported. Russia, which previously supplied low-cost fuel to Lithuania, has raised its oil prices, causing a strain on the Lithuanian economy.

Lithuania depends on the Ignalina nuclear power plant (*pictured above*) to supply its industries with the necessary power. However, the plant is old and similar in construction to the Chernobyl plant in Ukraine, which exploded in 1986. Although Lithuanians are skeptical about the safety of the Ignalina plant, it remains their main source of energy.

LIFE AFTER THE SOVIET UNION

The breakup of the Soviet Union in 1991 severely disrupted the economy of Lithuania. The Soviet Union had previously supplied Lithuania with heavily subsidized supplies of raw materials as well as guaranteed markets for the goods manufactured in Lithuania.

However, Lithuania has had considerable international support for its economic reform. It gained membership of the International Monetary Fund (IMF) and World Bank in April 1992. The European Bank for Reconstruction and Development, the World Bank, and the IMF guaranteed loans in 1993 to bolster the economy.

In June 1995, Lithuania signed the Europe Agreement with the European Union to become a member of the EU by the year 2000. Meanwhile, the European Union has provided considerable encouragement as well as financial support. Assistance has been concentrated in four core areas: sector restructuring in the key areas of agriculture, finance, labor, and privatization; infrastructure development; human resources development; and regional development programs.

AGRICULTURE AND FISHING

Lithuania has always been agriculturally self-sufficient. Lithuanians currently consume only 60 percent of the food they grow and are able to export the rest. Of a total land area of 16 million acres (6.5 million hectares), 8.6 million acres (3.5 million hectares) are used for agricultural purposes. The most important branch of the farming industry is livestock. Cattle, sheep, pigs, and chickens provide meat, eggs, and dairy products for export.

Wheat, barley, and oats are grown in the western and central part of the country, and potatoes and sugar beets are also important products. Flax is an important product of the eastern part of the country. This plant is used to make cloth.

The fishing industry is also profitable. Herring, cod, and flounder are brought in from the Baltic Sea, the Barents Sea, and the Atlantic Ocean. Carp and eel come from Lithuania's inland lakes and ponds.

Lithuania's dairy industry provides milk, cream, cheese, and yoghurt for local consumption and export.

The Sigma electronic factory in Vilnius.

Lithuania's most important natural resources are gravel, construction sand, quartz sand, dolomite, clay, limestone, brick clay, and mineral water.

INDUSTRIES

The main branches of industry are food processing, timber, oil processing, machinery, construction materials, chemicals, and light industry. The food processing industry is primarily based on local meat and dairy supplies. Other food industries are the production and packing of sugar, bread, confectionery, alcohol, beer, tobacco, and vegetable oil.

Vilnius and Kaunas are industrial centers, with textile mills producing knitwear, linen, cotton and silk fabrics, carpets, stockings, leather goods, and footwear. Substantial amounts of these products are exported to other European countries. Siauliai, the fourth largest Lithuanian city, is an industrial center involved in the production of precision lathes, television parts and components, computers, and bicycles. Raw materials are imported almost exclusively from the former Soviet Union, and most of the end products are exported to the Russian market.

Lithuania produces television and audio equipment, refrigerators, vacuum cleaners, electric engines, drills, and some agricultural machinery. The construction materials industry is based on local raw materials and satisfies local needs in cement, brick, glass, roof materials, thermal insulation, and nonmetal materials. Cement and bricks are exported. The chemical industry, based entirely on imported raw materials, specializes in fertilizers, plastics, household chemicals, and rubber products. Local timber is processed mainly for local consumption.

PRIVATIZATION

In the 1950s and 1960s, the Soviets forced the collectivization of agriculture and industry. One of the major changes brought about by independence was the privatization of these state-owned enterprises and cooperatives.

Lithuania's successful privatization program has been achieved by the use of vouchers, which were issued to all citizens in 1991 on the basis of age. The vouchers can be exchanged for ownership in former state assets. These investment decisions are now often handled by professional managers.

Some of the agricultural cooperatives were split into small farms, while the rest remained collectively owned and are now known as "communes." In 1993, family farms accounted for 69 percent of agricultural production. The family farms average only 10–17 acres (4–7 hectares) in size.

Of the remaining 1,500 agricultural communes, 700 are now relatively prosperous. The rest are expected to go bankrupt, merge with other cooperatives, or split into private farm holdings.

THE AMBER COAST

Lithuania was once known as the Amber Coast because of its great deposits of amber, a fossilized tree resin valued for its beauty. Amber can be found scattered like pebbles along the beaches of the Baltic shores. For centuries it has been a source of wealth for the Balts, who traded it as far away as Egypt. Tutankhamun's tomb included jewelry made with amber. A peculiarity of the stone is that before hardening the resin attracts insects, which become trapped inside. One can sometimes look closely at a piece of amber and see inside a perfectly preserved mosquito or gnat from long ago.

TRANSPORTATION

Transportation in Lithuania is good and continuously improving. The Via Baltica, the highway that links Lithuania to Latvia and Estonia in the north and Poland in the south, runs through Lithuania via Kaunas. Major airlines arrive daily at Vilnius Airport. Overall, aviation carried about one million passengers and 5,000 tons of freight in 1993.

In the same period, the railways carried some 25 million people and 30 million tons of freight. Railway lines crisscross the country. Future plans focus on the Kaunas freight and passenger terminal, which is planned to be the hub of rail links between Latvia, Russia, Belarus, and Poland.

Klaipeda, the largest ice-free port in the Baltic states, transships a considerable variety of goods, such as machinery, oil, coal, cement, grain, sugar, fish, and other foods. Some 80 percent of transit traffic comes from trade with Belarus and Ukraine. Klaipeda has a bulk terminal, a commercial port, a fishing port, and three ship repair yards.

Such integrated transport systems, a key geographical position, and the historical relationship with the former Soviet republics are making Lithuania of considerable interest to Western companies. IBM, DHL, Rank Xerox, Olivetti, and Minolta have come to Lithuania. German car giant Volkswagen Audi has opened a second showroom, the Swiss Vast group has opened a chain of stores across the country, Scandinavian companies are initiating joint ventures, and a German concern is preparing to manufacture tractors near Kaunas.

Lithuanian Airlines provides a comprehensive service to the east and west.

40

THE WORKING LIFE

Workers at one of the shipyards in Klaipeda.

In 1993, the working-age population of Lithuania was 2.1 million, of whom 1.9 million were in active employment. In 1995, 5.1 percent of the labor force was registered as unemployed. Women comprised more than half of all unemployed.

The main areas of employment in Lithuania are manufacturing and industry (employing around 24 percent of the labor force); agriculture, hunting, and forestry (23 percent); and transportation, storage, and communications (6 percent). The government and state-owned enterprises employ over 46 percent of the workers.

Post-independence Lithuanians have a 40-hour week. There is a national minimum annual leave of 28 days. Extended annual leave of 35 days is granted to the disabled and people under 18 years. Employees working under greater physical or mental strain, those in high risk professions, and certain others are given 58 days annual leave. Childcare leave is available for parents with children under 3 years old.

LITHUANIANS

INDO-EUROPEAN SETTLERS ARRIVED in the Baltic region in around 2,500 B.C. They organized into several tribes, and in the course of time these tribes merged to form today's ethnic Lithuanians. The tribes were the Lithuanians, Samogitians (or Zemaitians), Jotvings, Semigallians, Curonians, and Selonians. The Jotvings lived in the Suvalkija region, the Semigallians and Selonians lived in the north, the Curonians inhabited the far west, and the Samogitians inhabited the Zemaitija region. Today these tribes and their descendants—the people of Lithuania and Latvia—are referred to as Balts. This term was derived from the name of the Baltic Sea and was first used during the 19th century.

From the 13th century, Lithuania was settled by other nationalities as well, including Poles, Germans, Russians, and Tatars. At the beginning of the 14th century many Jews settled in Lithuania, where they found refuge from persecution in other European countries. In the second half of the 18th century, Orthodox Christians seeking sanctuary from religious persecution settled in Lithuanian villages.

The character of today's Lithuanians has been influenced by decades of intense Soviet repression. Many talented and educated Lithuanians fled the country in 1944, and many more died under German and Soviet occupation. In spite of a concerted attempt to stamp out Lithuanian culture and identity, the Lithuanians have held on to their traditions and still point proudly to the historical greatness of their country. They feel themselves to be the natural leaders of the Baltic region, although they may also feel some apprehension about what the future holds for their struggling new country.

Opposite: **A Lithuanian girl wearing flowers and a necklace of amber.**

Below: **Young men at a construction site.**

The population of Lithuania is around 3.8 million. The largest population group in Lithuania is the ethnic Lithuanians (80 percent). Next are the Russians (8.9 percent), of whom almost 90 percent live in the urban areas. Poles form the third largest ethnic group (7.3 percent). Most of the Poles reside in Vilnius and southeastern Lithuania. People of other ethnic groups are few: Ukrainians (1.7 percent), Belorussians (1.3 percent), Latvians (0.4 percent), and Jews (0.3 percent). Tatars, Gypsies, and Germans make up another 0.1 percent.

RUSSIANS

Lithuanian Russians mostly came to Lithuania after World War II, when Lithuania underwent rapid industrialization. Most of them belong to the Russian Orthodox Church. There is some resentment toward Russians among ethnic Lithuanians, although the problem is not as acute as it is in the other Baltic states, where the percentage of Russians is much higher.

Ethnic Russian singers at a Lithuanian music festival.

POLES

The Polish presence in Lithuania dates back to the Middle Ages, when Grand Duke Jogaila's marriage to the Polish princess Jadwiga joined the two countries. Many upper-class Lithuanians adopted the Polish language and Polish customs, and the line between the two groups became blurred. Until World War II, ethnic Lithuanians were a small minority in Vilnius, behind the Poles and the Jews. Many important Polish cultural figures came from Vilnius, such as writers Czeslaw Milosz and Adam Mickiewicz, and Jozef Pilsudski, the ruler of Poland between the wars.

As a result of the historical conflict between the two countries over Vilnius, many Lithuanians fear that the Poles want to reclaim Vilnius. Fear of Lithuanian nationalism in turn made many Poles support the Soviets during the independence struggle, another factor which has not eased relations. It is possible that the Catholic Church, which commands the allegiance of both groups, may help to ease these tensions.

Approximately 2.9 million Lithuanians live outside their homeland, of which more than 150,000 live in Russia and Eastern European countries. The largest external Lithuanian community in the world is in Marquette Park, a suburb of Chicago.

Polish Lithuanians in traditional dress.

THE JERUSALEM OF THE NORTH

Jews began settling in Lithuania in the 14th century, when they were invited by Grand Duke Vytautus. By the 18th century, Lithuania was considered to be one of the most important centers of Jewish culture in the world. Vilnius was known as "the Jerusalem of the North" because of its large Jewish population—30 percent of the population of Vilnius—and large number of synagogues and Hebrew schools. Jews made up 7.6 percent of the total Lithuanian population. Later in the 18th century, Vilnius was a center of Jewish Orthodox resistance to the Hasidic movement then sweeping Eastern Europe, and before World War II Vilnius was the center of Yiddish publishing.

The Jewish community was almost entirely destroyed by the Nazis during the German occupation of Lithuania. More than 130,000 Vilnius Jews died, and the rich Jewish culture that had flourished in Vilnius since the Middle Ages was wiped out. The Nazis interred and exterminated Jews

TATARS

The Tatars, also known as Mongols, came to Lithuania during the time of Vytautas the Great, who was their protector. About 50,000–100,000 Tatars moved to Lithuania during this time. Their main occupation was fighting in battles against enemies of Lithuania, since the Tatars are renowned for their valor in battle. In return, Lithuanian rulers gave them protection and religious freedom. Later, the Tatars took up agriculture, animal husbandry, and processing animal skins. A famous Lithuanian Tatar was General Maciej Sulkiewicz, who headed the Cabinet of Ministers of the Republic of Crimea in 1918.

at Fort Nine, the only Nazi concentration camp in Lithuania, a few miles outside Kaunas. Jews from all over Europe were herded here to await execution. The prison cells still exist, and there is now a museum and a monument to the victims on the spot.

Today only two communities of Jews remain, one in Vilnius and the other in Kaunas. In 1989 there were only 12,400 Jews in the entire country. Many of those Jews who were not killed in the Holocaust have joined the steady flow of emigres away from the Baltic states. The desire to emigrate is encouraged by memories of Lithuanian participation in the Holocaust—the initial massacres in Lithuania were conducted entirely by Lithuanians without direct German involvement—and by perceptions of contemporary anti-Semitism. The Lithuanians, on their side, accuse the Jews of supporting the Soviet regime that took control of the country in 1940. It is true that many Jews supported the Soviet regime. However, once in power, the Jewish Communists indiscriminately deported people of all religions. In fact, a higher proportion of Jews than Balts was deported to Siberia in 1940–41.

TRADITIONAL DRESS

The Lithuanian national dress dates from the early 19th century. Dress differs considerably from one area to another in ornamentation and color. From the early 20th century, the national dress, particularly for women, has been influenced by urban traditions. Today national dress is usually worn by the participants of folk music and dance concerts and at religious and ethnic festivals and processions. Most are produced commercially according to designs drawn by professionals. However, the tradition of making one's own is again becoming popular.

Men's dress consists of a shirt, trousers, vest, lightweight coat, greatcoat, sheepskin coat, headdress, and footwear. Shirts are full-sleeved and made of thick linen, with a cotton standup collar embroidered in black and red. Before the 20th century, trousers were made of homespun linen, wool, or cotton. Winter trousers are dark colored, and summer ones are white or white on blue. They are tied with a sash around the waist. Strips of cord or leather are appliquéd to the edging, cuffs, collars, and pockets of coats and jackets, which are worn over vests. Many kinds of caps are worn by men in the rural areas, but in warm weather straw hats are preferred.

There are several kinds of traditional footwear in the countryside, but the most striking is perhaps the solid wooden shoes called *klumpes* ("KLOOM-pus").

In the past, the clothes of a Lithuanian woman reflected her industry, accomplishment, and taste. Traditional woman's dress consists of a skirt, blouse, bodice, apron, and sash. Outer garments are a sheepskin coat and a scarf.

Women of the Aukstaitija region prefer light colors, particularly white. Their skirts are mostly checked, and the apron has horizontal red patterns at the bottom. The background of the apron is usually checked, striped, or patterned in cat-paw motifs. The front of the blouse, sleeves, collars, and cuffs are embellished with red stripes.

The Zemaitian women's attire includes several articles of sharply contrasting colors—a tailored bodice, a vertically striped skirt, and an apron. Shawls are worn over the head and shoulders. Klumpes are the typical Zemaitian footwear.

Amber necklaces are an important accessory for every woman wearing traditional dress.

Women's traditional clothes in the Klaipeda region are dark in color, and the blouses have a gathered neckline. The bottom portion of sleeves, the cuffs, and a wide band below the shoulders have designs such as clovers, tulips, or oak leaves. Their sashes and stoles have intricate patterns. The stole is made of two panels with a narrow lengthwise insertion embroidered with white plant motifs. Almost all women have a decorative handbag called a *delmonas* ("dayl-MOH-nus"), which is fastened at the front or side of the waistband.

LIFESTYLE

LITHUANIANS HAVE RETAINED many features of their traditional lifestyle in spite of the Communist occupation, which discouraged national traditions. Due to modernization, emigration to foreign lands, urbanization, and higher levels of education, some events have been simplified and are practiced only as rituals. Their original meaning has been forgotten. However, more and more Lithuanians are trying to bring the traditional lifestyle back into their everyday lives.

Opposite: **Young boys in the Old Quarter of Vilnius.**

Left: **Country women take a break for lunch in the fields.**

RURAL LIVING

Rural living has always been an important part of the Lithuanian way of life. Today, many of the old Soviet collectives have been broken up into small plots of land, much as the land was distributed during the prosperous period earlier this century, and rural Lithuanians are returning to a more traditional lifestyle.

Some city dwellers are also turning towards self-sufficiency on the land. During the Soviet era, small plots of land measuring 6,460 square feet (600 square meters) were provided for company and factory workers. Densely planted with fruit trees, vegetables, herbs, and flowers, they sprawl around the towns and cities. Some people built rough weekend shacks on their allotments. Since independence, planning permission has been loosely enforced and more solid, brick-built houses are appearing on these plots.

A LITHUANIAN INTERIOR

The interior and furniture of Lithuanian houses are designed for the needs of domestic life. The colors and textures of different woods are used to good advantage, giving the house a warm, cozy look. Sunlight filtering onto walls and ceilings shows off the wood's coarse, natural textures.

Lithuanians use moderate amounts of bright colors in their decoration of furniture, curtains, paintings, flooring, and linens. The furniture includes chests for fabrics and clothes, cupboards for food, utensils and clothes, and tables, benches, chairs, and beds. The chests, cupboards, and wardrobes are decorated with paintings, printed ornaments, or relief carvings.

Altars, religious icons, and statues are also used to adorn the interior of homes. Paintings on wooden panels or canvas depicting saints and scenes from the Bible are hung on walls.

In addition to the house, farms have barns for cows, pigs, poultry, and fodder, as well as granaries, a well, a sauna, a kitchen garden, and an orchard.

Farms are encircled with maple and linden trees. Oaks, considered to be the most beautiful trees, are planted at the front, birch trees near the barns, and rowan trees at the fringes of the property. Almost every house has a cross erected by the roadside. A flower garden is a traditional part of every Lithuanian house and farm.

During the long, dark winters, fish may be caught in the frozen lakes, and licensed professionals hunt wild game. When spring melts the snow, the swamps rise and the rivers burst their banks. Some houses on the delta of the Nemunas River are built on stilts to escape the flood waters. The arrival of the stork signifies the return of spring.

In summer, the country areas are filled with visitors from the city. Some city children spend the whole summer with relatives in the country. Weekend visitors go home with baskets and bags full of wild berries.

The summer harvest is hard work. Agricultural machinery is limited and out of date, and horses and carts are still evident in most of Lithuania. Scythes and pitchforks are used as much as they ever were. The unpredictable weather affects the harvest, and nobody is sure what will appear in the shops. This, coupled with the uncertain economy, means that Lithuanians view their patch of land as insurance against hunger and deprivation.

Lithuanians love birds. A birdhouse, or a cartwheel fixed to a tree or rooftop for the stork to nest in, is a ubiquitous part of the rural scene. Houses where birds make nests are considered safe resting places for travelers because the birds indicate that a good person lives there. Swallows nesting under the eaves are believed to protect the house against lightning.

URBAN LIFE

Sixty-nine percent of Lithuanians live in cities and towns. Around 40 percent live in the five largest cities—Vilnius, Kaunas, Klaipeda, Siauliai, and Panevezys.

After World War II, the population of the cities grew steadily as the cities were rebuilt and new industries developed. Today, the housing is a mix of houses and apartment blocks.

The Soviet regime built the huge apartment blocks that now surround almost every town in the Baltic region. These mass-produced and badly assembled concrete towers are very different from the attractive, historic city centers that tourists visit. Faced with a lack of housing, families live in cramped accommodation, sometimes with members of their extended family, or even sharing a kitchen and bathroom with other families in communal apartments. Street crime is increasing in the cities, and car theft is common. Still, the situation is better than that in many parts of the former Soviet Union. Public transportation in the cities is well developed, with some 50 bus lines and 20 streetcar lines in Vilnius. Lithuania has the most advanced telephone system in the former Soviet Union, and unlike some cities in neighboring countries, it is safe to drink the tap water.

Many Lithuanians live in high-rise apartments built during the Soviet era.

54

THE ROLE OF WOMEN

Lithuania was the first country in Europe to define the rights of women not simply as mothers or potential mothers, by a law introduced in 1529. This was the result of a matrilineal tradition in the ancient tribes and a society in which men were absent during long periods of war. The Statute of Lithuania of 1529 established the principle of individual legal responsibility and equality for women in the eyes of the law, irrespective of religion or marital status.

In present-day Lithuania, women can be found working in all occupations. Wage discrimination on the grounds of sex, age, race, nationality, or political convictions is illegal.

Lithuanian women have excelled in politics, literature, and archaeology. Marija Gimbutas achieved fame as an archaeologist, ethnologist, linguist, and author of numerous books. Among her published books are: *Ancient Symbolism in Lithuanian Folk Art*, *The Language of the Goddess*, *The Civilization of the Goddess*, and *The World of Old Europe*.

Women were active participants in the pro-independence movement, attending rallies such as this one in 1990. After independence, the first prime minister of Lithuania was a woman, Kazimiera Prunskiene.

An extended family outside their house in the country.

THE FAMILY

Today, most Lithuanian families are nuclear families, consisting of a married couple and their children.

Prior to World War II, many extended families, composed of grandparents, parents, children, uncles, aunts, and their children, lived and worked together as units in the villages. Often servants and other non-relatives lived in the house and were treated as part of the family. Today extended families are sometimes found, both in the cities and countryside, as a result of the housing shortage.

Traditionally, a woman goes to live with her husband's family when she marries, and daughters-in-law are readily accepted as members of the family.

BIRTH

It is still thought that evil spirits and improper behavior can harm an unborn baby or the expectant mother. For this reason, pregnant women have to observe a number of restrictions. At the same time, family, friends, and neighbors—in fact the whole village—protect and indulge the whims and fancies of the expectant mother.

Childbirth is shrouded in secrecy, and people talk of expectant mothers and the actual birth by using euphemisms, such as "The oven fell apart at Petra's," or "It is a joyous day at Antana's."

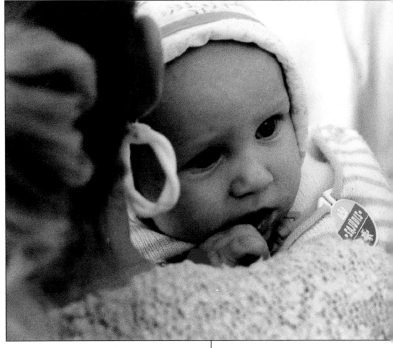

Even this baby is a patriotic Lithuanian, wearing a badge with the national colors.

The birth of a child is considered a blessing. Soon after the birth, the married women among the new parents' relatives and neighbors visit the mother and child. Each visitor brings a symbolic gift. No visitor comes empty-handed, as that is considered to jeopardize the child's good fortune. In many areas, it is customary to bring an omelette or a buckwheat loaf.

The child's christening is held two or more weeks after the birth. Godmothers and godfathers play an important role in the christening. The selection of these godparents is considered crucial because it is thought that the child absorbs their temperaments and habits. This process ties families together, as the godparents take on part of the responsibility of raising the child.

CHILDHOOD RITUALS

It is through ritual introduction to adult responsibilities that the young are considered to have come of age.

The baking of her first loaf is the proof of a girl's coming of age and marks the reaching of puberty. On a Friday evening, the mother hands flour to her daughter. The daughter mixes the dough and leaves it to ferment overnight. On Saturday morning, the girl kneads the dough and allows it to rise. She lights the oven, forms the loaves, incises a cross on the top of the first and puts the loaves in the oven. When they are done, she removes them. The bread is eaten that day by her family.

In rural areas, fathers teach their sons how to harness and unharness horses, yoke and unyoke oxen, and plow their first furrow.

The mother takes some of her daughter's first loaf of bread to the local sauna to treat her neighbors and boasts of her new helper who has come of age.

Ice cream—one of the small pleasures of childhood in Lithuania.

58

GOING TO SCHOOL

A new national education system was introduced in Lithuania in 1990. Education is compulsory from 6 years of age until 16, and it is free of charge at all levels. General schools go from 6 to 14 years, and secondary schools go from 15 to 17 years. Lithuanian is the main language of instruction, although there are schools at which classes are taught in Russian, Polish, or Yiddish, with some schools offering classes in two or more languages. There are 15 institutions of higher education in Lithuania, including Vilnius University, Vytautas Magnus University in Kaunas, Vilnius Technical University, and the Lithuanian Academy of Sciences.

Adult literacy is very high—99.2 percent for men and 97.8 percent for women. In 1992, 22 percent of government spending went towards education.

Children and their parents attending school on the first day of class.

The bride and groom
leaving the church.

WEDDINGS

Modern Lithuanian weddings are full of humor and good-natured teasing. Although they have been simplified, they retain the main elements of traditional weddings.

After the civil ceremony and the wedding in the church, the wedding party heads for the bride's home for the feast. The way is barred by the bride's family and friends with ropes of garlands and flowers. The last of the garlands is stretched across her parents' gate. The groom's friends buy their passage with sweets and a bottle of whisky. They also distribute sweets to children along the way.

The bride's parents meet the newlyweds at their threshold with bread, salt, and wine glasses filled with water.

Inside, the seats for the bride and groom are adorned with flowers and garlands, but they are already occupied by neighbors dressed as gypsies, a matchmaker, a bride (a man in disguise), and a bridegroom (a woman in disguise). Both groups start haggling over the price of the seats, and after much banter and laughter the seats are sold for a bottle of whisky.

The food is deliberately made bitter, and on the first bite the guests start singing a traditional song: "Bitter, bitter is the food. It will be sweet when the bridegroom kisses the bride." The guests then volunteer lots of instructions to the bridegroom on how to do it well.

A very important part is played by the matron of honor, who is usually a married woman closely related to the bride. She remains next to the bride and groom, makes sure all the customs are followed, and acts as a symbolic guard to the bridal pair to ensure no evil damages their health and fertility.

The bride says goodbye to her parents, family, garden, neighbors, and friends, and asks for forgiveness if she has ever hurt them by word or deed. This is a rather sorrowful part of the celebration, accompanied by the bride's family's *raudos* ("RAO-dohs"), or farewell songs.

Parents prepare dowry chests for their daughters well in advance. These chests are made from the wood of a tree in which storks nest, so as to bring luck and fertility. The chests are filled with jewelry, documents, letters, money, a rue wreath, medicinal herbs, clothes for the firstborn child, linen, bed cloths, rolls of fabric, woven sashes, and other handmade articles. The size and beauty of her dowry chest is an indication of the bride's wealth, taste, and industry.

EXECUTING THE MATCHMAKER

Arranging marriages with the help of the matchmaker was once widely practiced in Lithuania, but today the young choose their own life partners and matchmakers rarely play a part. Therefore, matchmakers are only characters acted out at weddings, to lend fun to the atmosphere.

A wedding tradition that has continued is the mock execution of the matchmaker. The bride's friends and siblings decide that the matchmaker had exaggerated the description of the groom's looks and possessions, so they decide to execute the matchmaker. The sentence varies—he may be condemned to be burned by water, or frozen to death on the stove, or to be sent away to a hay loft with all the girls of the neighborhood. He accepts his sentence and asks to be allowed to say goodbye to all the ladies. He then smears his face with soot and tries to kiss every woman and girl in the house. The wittier the matchmaker, the funnier is his "execution." In the end, the bride's mother takes pity on the poor man, and as a sign of her forgiveness throws a towel across his shoulders. The matchmaker is thus saved, and the guests hang a dummy instead.

HEALTH

Until 1940, health care was provided by both state and private facilities. The Soviets introduced comprehensive state-funded health care. In 1991, after the establishment of Lithuanian independence, a National Health Concept was adopted, which criticized Soviet health care and called for extensive reform of the system. A national health care insurance plan covers all residents. The 1992 constitution guarantees the right of all citizens to receive old-age pensions, disability pensions, and assistance in the event of unemployment, sickness, or widowhood.

There is about one doctor for every 250 people in Lithuania. Doctors are well educated, but they are forced to work with a limited supply of medical instruments, materials, and medicines.

THE ELDERLY

Great respect is shown to elders in Lithuanian society. A younger person would respectfully address an elderly person as grandmother, grandfather, uncle, or aunty, never by his or her name.

In modern Lithuania, where both parents work, grandparents take care of their grandchildren. Grandparents may move in with their children and grandchildren. This gives the grandparents the opportunity to teach the third generation about Lithuanian customs, beliefs, traditions, folk tales, crafts, games, dances, and music, and to tell stories of their ancient heritage and mythology.

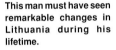

This man must have seen remarkable changes in Lithuania during his lifetime.

FUNERALS

In villages, the dead lie in state at home for three days. In towns and cities, they lie in the funeral parlor for two days. The footpath in front of the house or funeral parlor is strewn with pieces of spruce branches.

The dead person is dressed in his or her best clothes, and the body is laid in a room with the walls adorned with beautiful woven bedspreads. A cross, some pictures of saints, and two burning candles are placed at the head. Wreaths and ribbons inscribed with words of condolence are hung on walls or placed on the sides of the coffin.

Family and friends keep vigil throughout the days and nights. Silence is observed as much as possible, as it is thought that though the spirit separates from the body at death, it does not leave the house until the corpse is carried away. In the evenings the neighbors gather to pray and sing hymns written by local poets. After the prayers, a funerary meal is served. If the family owns a pig, it is killed for this meal.

Wooden grave markers in a Lithuanian cemetery.

In southeastern Lithuania, the tradition of raudos at funerals still survives. Laments, spoken or sung by professionals or relatives, express the sorrow of the living and the sad plight of the children left behind, as well as recalling the good deeds of the deceased.

In the country, the dead are usually buried in the morning. Before closing the lid, a cross is burnt onto the lid with a hallowed candle. It is traditional to give the dead person a last kiss. After the coffin is laid in the grave, everyone throws in a handful of soil. Throwing flowers into the grave is a new custom. After burial, a cross is pressed onto the top of the mound and wreaths and flowers are laid on it.

RELIGION

THE LITHUANIANS WERE THE LAST Europeans to renounce their ancient beliefs and rites. The country converted to Christianity only in the 14th century. Today the main religion of Lithuania is Roman Catholicism. While most ethnic Lithuanians and virtually all Poles are Roman Catholics, there are also small pockets of Lutherans, Calvinists, and some other Protestant denominations. Adherents of Russian Orthodoxy and the Old Believers (Old Ritualists) are mostly Russians. There are some Tatars, who are Muslim, and a small Jewish community.

Opposite: **A Catholic priest conducting mass at the chapel inside the Gates of Dawn, part of the old fortifications in Vilnius. The chapel houses a Renaissance painting of Our Lady of Vilnius that is believed to be miraculous.**

Below: **Catholic girls at a church service.**

There are still a few Lithuanians who practice the ancient religion, and many others who combine some of the old traditions with Christianity. These people are celebrating the Day of Gediminas around the time of the autumn equinox.

PRE-CHRISTIAN RELIGION

The religion of the ancient Lithuanians was based on animism—the belief that all things have a spirit. Ancient Lithuanians worshiped objects and natural phenomena. Cults devoted to forests and fire were widespread. There were sacred fields and forests that no one was allowed to enter or work in. Certain kinds of trees, such as oaks and pines, held special powers. Up until the 18th century, Catholic officials were still chopping

down sacred oak trees in an attempt to suppress Lithuanians' pagan (non-Christian) beliefs. Lithuanians have retained a reverence for nature and a belief in the sanctity of all living things, and elements of the ancient religion survive to this day through legends, folk tales, exorcisms, and songs.

The prehistoric hunters and farmers of Lithuania had a matriarchal tribal system, and their religious imagery was feminine. The later patriarchal tribal and feudal systems saw the introduction of male gods and the decline of the importance of goddesses, although some goddesses remained in the Lithuanian pantheon of gods together with masculine deities.

Places of worship were outdoors, usually in a sacred grove of trees, on a hillside, or near a holy stream. There were special people, usually men, who performed religious rituals. These men were similar to priests, the wise men and leaders of a community. Sacrifice of animals—calves, pigs, sheep, goats, and chickens—was common and continued into the 1500s. Human sacrifice was not practiced except after a victorious battle, when the leader of the enemy would be sacrificed to thank the gods.

The ancient Lithuanians had a strong belief in the afterworld. The dead were buried with household objects and food for the afterworld, and warriors and leaders were buried with their horses. Grand Duke Algirdas was cremated with 18 horses in 1377.

THE LITHUANIAN GODS

The ancient Lithuanian religion was polytheistic, meaning that many gods were worshiped. The pantheon of Lithuanian gods is rich and diverse. The god of bright daylight, Dievas, was the supreme deity and was a kind, gentle, and wise god. The most popular god was Perkunas, the god of thunder. He was master of the atmosphere and the "waters" of the sky, as well as fertility, human morality, and justice. Under the influence of Christianity, Perkunas was transformed into the Lord of Heaven. Velnias was the guardian of wizards and sages. The goddess of forests was Medeina, and the goddess of hunting was Zvorune. There were female deities representing the sun, the moon, water, earth, and fertility. Other goddesses were responsible for the birth, life, and death of man, flora, and fauna. These deities took care that the continuity of life in the world be maintained through the continual flux of life and death.

CHRISTIANITY'S RUGGED ROAD

Christian teachings first reached Lithuania in the 11th and 12th centuries, but it took a while before they were accepted. In 1251, Mindaugas adopted Christianity in order to have Pope Innocent crown him king. Soon after, he reverted to his old ways and sacrificed a Christian princess to Perkunas, the god of thunder. A later attempt to introduce Catholicism was more successful: Jogaila converted to Roman Catholicism and made it the religion of his country in 1385, when he married Princess Jadwiga of Poland.

It was a difficult beginning, though. The first Christian church in Lithuania was near Kaunas. It had a roof that sloped steeply. According to legend, the roof did not slope when it was constructed. The god Perkunas so resented the presence of a Christian church that he engulfed it in a storm, which caused the church building to sink and so increased the slope of the roof!

A young woman being baptized by a Catholic bishop.

Protestantism—first Lutheranism and then Calvinism—came to Lithuania in the 16th century. In the 17th century, largely due to the efforts of the Jesuits, Lithuania was reclaimed by the Catholics. At this time a number of Old Believers (the Old Ritualists) settled in Lithuania, having fled from Russia to avoid persecution. Catholicism flourished in the 17th and 18th centuries. Many churches and monasteries were built, and the ranks of priests grew.

However, in 1795 a greater part of Lithuania was annexed to Russia, and the Catholic Church was restricted. In the 19th century the Catholic church was persecuted. Monasteries were closed down and churches were given over to the Russian Orthodox Church. From 1799 to 1915 the Russian Orthodox faith was the official religion in Lithuania, although the Lithuanians struggled to remain Catholic. The most prominent figure in the struggle to maintain the Lithuanian cultural identity was Bishop Motiejus Valancius. In time, the Russian authorities had to give in, and 1897 saw the lifting of the ban to build Catholic churches.

Under the Lithuanian Republic (1918–40), the Catholic Church regained its place as the official religion of the state. Direct ties with the Vatican were established in 1922. In 1926, the Lithuanian Church Province was created under direct subordination to the Pope, and relations with the Vatican were settled in 1927. The state also supported other religious communities, including other Christians as well as Muslims and Jews.

Lighting candles at a Catholic church service in Vilnius.

SOVIET REPRESSION

Lithuania's incorporation into the Soviet Union on June 15, 1940, caused major losses to all churches, including (to a lesser degree) the Russian Orthodox Church and the Old Believers. All the Catholic monasteries and 690 churches were closed down, and church lands were taken over by the state. Many churches became concert halls or museums—St. Casimir's, in Vilnius, was turned into a Museum of Atheism. Religious literature was restricted, and religious instruction banned. Those who attended church could find their careers in jeopardy, and their children would be banned from higher education.

Opposite: **One of the two Russian Orthodox monasteries in Vilnius.**

Below: **A traditional wooden church in the Zemaitija region.**

In this atmosphere of repression, religious practices were carried on secretly. A group of Catholic priests regularly published the *Chronicles of the Lithuanian Catholic Church,* which informed the world about repression and human rights violations.

The persecution of the churches came to an end in 1988. In 1990 the Act of the Restitution of the Catholic Church was promulgated, giving freedom of worship once more to all Lithuanians. Today about 80 percent of Lithuanians are Roman Catholic. Monasteries and convents have reopened. Workers are renovating churches. In 1989, the Catholic organization Caritas, the Lithuanian Catholic Teachers' Union, and the Catholic Action Center resumed their activities. In 1990 the Lithuanian Catholic Academy of Sciences was moved back to Lithuania from abroad.

THE RUSSIAN ORTHODOX CHURCH

In 1054, Christianity underwent a major east–west division into the Roman Catholic Church and the Greek Orthodox Church, which later came to Russia. The name of the church in Russia is the Russian Orthodox Church. The church is headed by the Patriarch of All Russia and does not recognize the Pope. Members of the church in Lithuania are almost exclusively Russians or other Slavs. There are 45 congregations governed by city and national church bodies, under the jurisdiction of the Patriarchate in Moscow.

THE OLD BELIEVERS

There are 51 religious congregations headed by the Supreme Pomorski Old Ritualists' Council in Vilnius. The Old Believers are a group that formed as the result of a schism in the Russian Orthodox Church in the 17th century. Many emigrated to the Baltic states, where there was more religious freedom. They have no priests or sacraments except baptism. Since 1971 they have been officially recognized by the council of the Russian Orthodox Church.

OTHER CHRISTIAN DENOMINATIONS

Lutheranism came to Lithuania in the early 1500s. Today there are tens of thousands of members of the Lutheran Church in Lithuania. There are 33 Lutheran congregations governed by the Consistory of the Evangelical Lutheran Church of Lithuania in Taurage, which has been a member of the Lutheran World Foundation since 1968. Together with the Reformed Evangelical Church it publishes the periodical *Lietuvos evangeliku kelias* (The Road of the Lithuanian Evangelics).

Other Christian denominations in Lithuania include the Reformed Evangelical Church, the Evangelical Baptists, the Evangelical Faith in the Spirit of Apostles, the Seventh Day Adventists, and the Eastern Rites Roman Catholics. Fifteen thousand Lithuanians are Calvinists. The Lutherans, Calvinists, and Evangelists are most heavily concentrated in the coastal region, mainly because of the strong German influence in this area.

ISLAM

Islam came to Lithuania in the 14th century from Crimea and Kazan, a town on the Volga River, through the Tatars.

For the last six centuries, the Tatars of Lithuania have maintained their ethnic identity as well as their religion. They live primarily within compact communities, where the mosque is the central focus of their lives.

There were altogether 48 mosques in the Grand Duchy of Lithuania from 1397 to the end of the 18th century. During the commemoration of the 500th anniversary of Vytautas the Great's death in 1930, the government of Lithuania built a mosque in Kaunas in recognition of the Tatars.

During the 50 years of Soviet occupation, Lithuanian Muslims, like other ethnic religious groups, were prevented from practicing their faith.

Now about 6,000 Tatar Muslims live in Lithuania. After World War II, they were joined by about 18,000 Muslims from other nations. Today the Muslim community numbers about 25,000. There are four major congregations of Muslims in Lithuania and they worship at the Raiziai Mosque in Vilnius (built in the late 19th century), the Kaunas Mosque (1930), the Nemezis Mosque (early 20th century), and the oldest existing mosque in the village of Keturiasdesimt Totoriu (1815). The lifting of religious repression since independence has opened the way for new mosques to be built.

Tatars at a mosque in the Vilnius region.

73

Crosses, chapels, and wooden carvings are traditionally erected as memorials at places where people have died. A modern adaptation of this practice can be found in the wooden carvings at Ablinga, a village that was burned with all its inhabitants by the Nazis.

CROSSES AND MINIATURE CHAPELS

As Christianity is the dominant religion in Lithuania, the sign of the cross plays an important role in the life of the Lithuanians. These crosses and miniature chapels are found on roadsides, in yards and on homes, on farmsteads, in graveyards, on hill slopes and hilltops, beside rivers and springs, near forests, in churchyards, and in town squares. Some crosses incorporate pre-Christian religious elements, such as the sun, moon, and snake. The crosses in Lithuania can be divided into two broad types: the pillar type, which has a concealed and scarcely noticeable crossbeam, and the cross-shaped type.

Crosses are built for various purposes. Crosses are erected in cemeteries and in places where accidents have occurred in remembrance of the dead. They are erected in villages, fields, and by the road in the hope that God will give blessings, grant a good harvest, and keep away epidemics, droughts, quarrels, and other misfortunes. Other occasions for erecting crosses include moving to a new home or farm, births, christenings, weddings, and times of success and misfortune in the family.

Miniature chapels are suspended from trees, nailed to homesteads, mounted on niches cut in tree trunks, or mounted on poles in fields and forests. Some are simple and others ornate. They are like miniature houses or little chapels showing a statue or statues within. In some areas it is customary to affix a chapel to a tree when there is a birth or a death in the family.

The Hill of Crosses near the city of Siauliai.

Crosses and miniature chapels are to be found at places that are believed to be haunted and at springs whose waters are thought to have healing powers. Miniature chapels dedicated to St. John the Baptist are erected near rivers and bridges. Village communities, small towns, religious fraternities, and youth organizations have their own crosses.

The variety of crosses is evident in the exceptionally rich ornamentation and mix of materials. Huge crosses, some reaching 10 feet (3 m) in height, are carved out of stone. Wooden crosses and miniature chapels have ornate iron decorations that incorporate smaller crosses, trumpeting angels, and other Christian symbols into designs of radiating wavy sunbeams, arrows, crescents, stylized pine trees, lilies, and tulips.

The best example of Lithuanian crosses is on the Hill of Crosses, just north of Siauliai, where thousands of crosses are mounted on a hill. The hill is not as tall as it once was. It was bulldozed by the Soviets three times, and each time new crosses would be brought to replace the old ones.

LANGUAGE

THE LITHUANIAN LANGUAGE BELONGS to the family of Indo-European languages. It is the oldest living language in Europe today and retains many archaic features. It uses the Latin alphabet with variations for special sounds. Lithuanian is spoken by some three million people in Lithuania and by another one million living abroad. Lithuania is also rich in dialects and regional accents. Other languages spoken in Lithuania include Russian (as the second language), Latvian, Polish, and Belorussian. The languages of commerce and business are English, German, and French.

Opposite: **A quiet spot to read a book.**

Below: **Public telephones in Vilnius.**

THE LITHUANIAN LANGUAGE

The Lithuanian language belongs to the Baltic branch of the great Indo-European family. It is related to most of the other languages of Europe and Western Asia, from India to Iceland. Its source is the extinct language of India called Sanskrit. The early Indo-European languages were spoken 5,000 years ago by people who settled in Ukraine, southern Russia, the Euphrates, the Rhine and Indus valleys, and around the Aral Sea.

The Baltic branch consists of Lithuanian, Latvian, the extinct Old Prussian language, and the extinct dialects of the Curonians, Semigallians, and Selonians. The Lithuanian and Latvian languages separated in the 5th–7th centuries A.D., with Lithuanian retaining more ancient features than Latvian.

Lithuanian storybooks and textbooks.

The Lithuanian Language

Of all the living languages in Europe today, Lithuanian is the most archaic and has most faithfully preserved the primitive features of Sanskrit. This has happened because Lithuanian was spoken by a people whose lifestyle was isolated for many centuries from the outside world by dense forests and impassable marshes.

A very great many Lithuanian words are used by Belorussians and Poles in the areas formerly inhabited by Lithuanians. A complete dictionary of the Lithuanian language, which is nearing completion, will consist of 20 volumes and will contain about 400,000 entries.

During the Soviet era, Russian increasingly displaced Lithuanian in the country's cultural, economic, administrative, and political life. Major government institutions operated entirely in Russian. In 1989, the government reinstated Lithuanian as the national language. Lithuanian had been written in the Cyrillic script, but after the proclamation of independence in 1990, the Lithuanian language reverted to the Latin alphabet.

Teaching Lithuanian language and literature was prohibited from 1861 to 1904, and again from 1940 to 1989.

PRONUNCIATION GUIDE

The Lithuanian language uses the Latin alphabet. There are 32 letters in the alphabet. Unique Lithuanian sounds are represented by special characters.

Vowels

a – as in *ah*	e – as in th*e*re	ė – as in m*a*ke	i – as in s*i*t
o – as in sh*o*t	u – as in sh*ou*ld	ū – oo as in tr*u*th	y – ee as in s*ee*

ą, ę, į, ų appear in special cases and are pronounced a bit longer.

Consonants: b, d, f, g, h, k, l, m, n, p, t, and v are pronounced almost as in English

c – ts as in ticke*ts*	č – ch as in *ch*in	s – as in *s*it	š – sh as in *sh*e
z – as in *z*oo	ž – as in vi*si*on	j – y as in *y*es	r – is always trilled

LITHUANIAN WISDOM AND ADVICE

Every nation has its treasure of proverbs, brief and popular statements of wisdom or advice. Called *patarle* ("PAH-tehr-lay") in Lithuanian, proverbs are easy to remember.

In traveling by word of mouth from person to person, proverbs often retain their deeper meaning but change in their manner of expression according to local circumstances. Thus the English proverb "A bird in the

Traditional wisdom, proverbs, riddles, and folk tales are passed on through word of mouth.

hand is worth two in the bush" appears in Lithuanian as "A sparrow in the hand is better than an elk in the woods" and "A sparrow in the palm is better than a crane on the roof."

Sometimes Lithuanians copied proverbs exactly, like the Sanskrit proverb "God has given teeth, God will give bread." At other times they expressed ideas in their own way. Thus the English proverb "You cannot get blood out of a stone" becomes "You cannot shatter a wall with your head."

How would you describe a gluttonous and lazy person? Lithuanians would say he or she "eats like a horse and works like a rooster." How about a man who is happy for no reason? He would be said to be "as happy as though he has found a bit of iron." Such Lithuanian sayings and maxims are full of humor and are used as tools to educate children. Looking for something? "Maybe you will find it in the dew!"

LITHUANIAN RIDDLES

Which tongue (language) is easiest for everyone?
The mother tongue.

A young lady in the bathhouse, her braids outside.
A carrot.

A dark table cloth covered with crumbs and a chunk of bacon.
The sky, stars, and moon.

Though it bends, it breaks not.
Smoke.

It burns without fire and beats without a stick.
The heart.

This devilish character is one of the strange and magical creatures who inhabit the world of Lithuanian stories and legends.

STORYTELLING

At parties and gatherings, storytelling is a popular form of entertainment. Popular legends are inhabited by devils, sorcerers, ghosts, and spirits. These stories are of pre-Christian origin. According to legends, people traveling in remote places and at odd hours might come across these beings. The outcome of such an encounter is sometimes happy and sometimes not.

If you find a piece of horse manure in the place of the new pipe that you bought last night, you can be sure that the traveler you traded with was no ordinary man, but a devil. If you left an infant out in the fields overnight by mistake, you might only find its bones the next morning and know that some spirits had been at work. Tame spirits were good, however, and carried riches and goods to their masters.

Short stories without endings and tales about animals are especially popular among children. Domestic and forest animals that behave like human beings inhabit these stories. Heroes are often aided by magical objects and heavenly or earthly helpers. There are also modern stories about clever hired hands, gullible landlords, and matchmakers. Often, stories are embellished with short, simple songs, as if a character in the story was singing it.

Mystical tales are common and are often the most artistic. In these stories, heroes battle dragons or free people who have been turned into swans or grass snakes. The tragic story of Zilvinas, the king of the grass snakes, his wife Egle, and their family is a relic of the ancient cult of the grass snake.

EGLE, QUEEN OF THE GRASS SNAKES

Once upon a time there was an old man and an old woman. They had 12 sons and three daughters. The youngest daughter's name was Egle, and she was the darling of the family. One summer evening, she went for a swim in the sea. When she finished her swim and came to change back to her clothes, she found a grass snake lying curled in her shirtsleeve. He said he would give her shirt back if she agreed to marry him. Egle promised to marry him.

In a few days, she left her parents' house with a retinue of grass snakes. On the shore of the sea she was met by a handsome young man who was actually the same grass snake that had lain curled in her shirtsleeve. They crossed in a boat to an island nearby, and from there they descended into a beautiful palace at the bottom of the sea where they celebrated their wedding. Life in the palace was blissful. Egle forgot her homeland altogether, for she was happy. She gave birth to three sons—Azuolas (Oak), Uosis (Ash), and Berzas (Birch)—and lastly a daughter, Drebule (Aspen).

Nine years passed. Her oldest son asked her where her parents were and said he would like to visit them. Egle remembered her family again and wanted to go to see them, but her husband Zilvinas would not let her go because he was afraid she would not come back. He asked her to finish three tasks before she would be allowed to go.

The first task was to spin a bundle of silk. Egle spun and spun, but no matter how fast she worked, the bundle stayed the same size, so she asked a wise old woman for advice. The woman told her to throw the bundle into the fire. The silk burned away to reveal a toad that had been producing new silk as Egle spun. Her second task was to wear down iron shoes. Egle accomplished this task with the advice of the old woman, who told her to go to a foundry and ask the blacksmith to burn them down. Her third task was to bake a pie with just a sieve. But Zilvinas had given orders to hide all the water and cooking vessels in the kingdom. Egle could not even fetch water for the pie. On the advice of the old woman, she filled the holes of the sieve with baking dough, let it dry, and then brought some water from the river in it and made the pie.

Having accomplished all three tasks, she said goodbye to her husband on the seashore and, together with her children, departed for her parents' house. Before parting, Egle agreed that when she came back she would call her husband out of the sea by saying "Zilvinas, Zilvinas, if alive you are, milk white is the surf! If dead you are, blood red is the surf!"

Egle and her children had a very good time with her parents and siblings. When the time allotted for the visit was drawing to a close, Egle's brothers were unhappy and tried to get the password from her sons, so they could go and kill Zilvinas. Try as they would, they could not get it out of her sons. But the daughter, Aspen, blurted it out when they threatened to flog her.

When Egle and her children came back to the seashore and tried to call Zilvinas, they found the surf rolling blood red to the shore, and heard Zilvinas's voice coming from the bottom of the sea telling them of the betrayal. In her grief and pain, Egle turned her sons into strong trees—oak, ash, and birch. She turned her daughter into the quivering aspen and herself into the fir tree.

ARTS

THE ARTS AND CULTURAL SCENE in Lithuania is lively. Theaters, concert halls, and exhibition halls are open year round. During the summer months, many cultural festivals and drama and music competitions are held. There are many professional theaters, some state orchestras, and chamber groups in the major cities.

THEATER AND BALLET

Lithuania has a very long history of performance art, stemming from the ancient rituals and entertainments.

During the Soviet era, several Lithuanian plays were banned and the theater had to extol the virtues of Communism. Now that Lithuania is again independent, the theater enjoys much more freedom. In Vilnius, there are 14 theaters and concert halls. Kaunas has a branch of the National Philharmonic, a pantomime theater school, a puppet theater, and a youth chamber theater. The Lithuanian Theater of Youth is popular locally and known abroad.

Lithuanian ballet has a reputation of high quality. At the start of World War II, many fine dancers fled the country. However, the Academic Opera and Ballet Theater continued to operate in Vilnius through the Soviet years. It performed several Lithuanian pieces, and elements of folk dancing were skilfully worked into its repertoire.

Since independence, the ballet, like other art forms, is experiencing financial difficulty. The Soviet system financially supported a wide range of artists; this support no longer exists. However, there is hope that the ballet will continue to flourish as the country gains economic stability.

Above: **This ballerina is Svetlana Beriosova, a Lithuanian who achieved international fame.**

Opposite: **A street artist in Vilnius.**

Lithuanians of all ages come together to sing.

MUSIC

The Baltic states are famous for their choral singing. There are many professional and amateur choirs in Lithuania. Every five years there is a huge song festival called "Dainu Svente," where choirs, folk dance ensembles, and folk orchestras come from all over Lithuania to perform. The choir members number in the thousands and the audiences in tens or even hundreds of thousands—a large proportion of the population. There are also smaller song and dance festivals throughout the year. Under Soviet rule, these festivals were among the very few ways in which national feeling could be legally displayed, although several of the more patriotic songs were banned. The song festivals became a vehicle for nationalist sentiment, and the independence movement in the Baltic states has often been called the "Singing Revolution."

MUSIC FESTIVALS

May	Jazz festival, Birstonas
August	Pop music festival, Palanga
September	Griezyne folk music festival, Vilnius
	International pop music festival, Vilnius
Fall	Grok Jurgeli, folk music festival, Kaunas
October	Jazz festival, Vilnius
November	Italian opera week
	Gaida Baltica Music Festival
Every five years	Dainu Svente, traditional song festival

THE KANKLES

The southwestern region of Lithuania is the home of *kankles* ("KAHN-klis") music. The *kankles* is one of the most ancient string instruments in the Baltic countries. It had been on the verge of extinction, but was revived by a few enthusiasts just before World War II. The kankles is a kind of board zither with between five and 12 iron or natural fiber strings. It goes back at least 3,000 years and is native to the Baltic states. The word kankles means "the singing tree" and comes from an Indo-European word *qan* meaning "to sing" or "sound."

Kankles are thought to be associated with death. Lithuanians believe that in order to make sonorous kankles, the wood from which they are crafted has to be cut from a mature forest on the day that a loved one dies. As the household mourns, the wood acquires depth and soul. It is shaped like a small boat or coffin. Kankles are made by skilled master craftsmen and are not easy to find. There are also few musicians who know how to play the instruments, although a folk revival in the 1970s and 1980s has revived interest in traditional instruments.

Playing the kankles is very much like meditating and is thought to protect the musician from death, disease, and accidents. In general only men play the kankles, sometimes crafting their own instruments.

Lithuania has produced several composers of note, including M. K. Ciurlionis, choral composer Velio Tormis, and modernist Osvaldas Balakauskas. The National Philharmonic building in Vilnius houses the symphony orchestra and is also an umbrella organization for many other musical groups and soloists. There is an active live music scene, with bands performing rock, alternative music, and jazz.

In the absence of an alternative political structure, artists played an important leadership role in the Baltic independence movement. In Lithuania, a music professor, Vytautas Landsbergis, became the country's leader in 1990. Popular culture—particularly rock music, which was banned under Soviet rule—united many sections of the population and was used to express defiance during the 1980s.

A Lithuanian children's folk song and dance group, the Ugnele, was founded in 1954. Children aged 10–18 play and perform in this ensemble.

Weaving sashes is a traditional skill that is passed from mother to daughter as part of the daughter's coming of age rituals.

FOLK ART

Lithuanian folk art embraces a great variety of forms, from graphic art, religious art, and primitive painting to woodcarving, textiles, ceramics, and blacksmithing. Folk craft festivals and displays are a popular feature of Lithuania's cultural life.

Lithuania has an especially rich tradition of woodcarving. One branch of woodcarving was the carving of ritual wooden masks. These carvings have preserved some elements of ancient sorcery practices. Their most distinctive feature is folk humor and satire. Wooden crosses are another important folk art. They are often covered with ancient pre-Christian symbols. A more modern example of Lithuanian woodcarving skill is the wooden memorial sculptures commemorating the 41 residents of the village of Ablinga, which was burnt with all its inhabitants by the Nazis. In the field where Ablinga formerly stood, about 25 miles (40 km) from Klaipeda, a large wooden sculpture has been erected for each one of the dead.

TWO LITHUANIAN ARTISTS

M. K. CIURLIONIS Mikalojus Konstantinas Ciurlionis (1875–1911) was born in 1875 in the Dzukija region. Before he died at the age of 36, he almost single-handedly founded modern Lithuanian culture through his work as a painter, composer, and organizer of cultural events.

Both in painting and music, Ciurlionis was a pioneer and founder of new forms. He composed many works that are still performed, including the first Lithuanian symphony, *In the Forest*.

After establishing himself as a composer, Ciurlionis took up painting, believing that there were certain emotions that were better expressed in shapes and colors than in music. In his painting he created a mystical universe with motifs from Lithuanian folklore. He was among those who initiated the annual Lithuanian Art Exhibition in Vilnius in 1907.

PETRAS KALPOKAS The works of this Lithuanian artist belong to the period of the formation of Lithuania's national fine arts. He took deep interest in the first Lithuanian Art Exhibition in 1907 and was an active participant of other art exhibitions. He took part in various fields of art, producing paintings, frescos, and cartoons. His major works, however, were landscape and portrait paintings. He taught painting at the Kaunas School of Art and at the Institute of Decorative and Applied Arts.

Painted in 1903, this work by Ciurlionis is from the "Funeral" cycle. Ciurlionis was a mystic who saw nature as an inexhaustible source of beauty.

Flowers have been placed in front of a statue of the poet Salomeja Neris.

LITERATURE

Lithuania's first pieces of writing date back to the Middle Ages. They were not in Lithuanian but in Old Church Slavic, Latin, and Polish.

The first book in the Lithuanian language, the Protestant Catechism, was printed in 1547. The Lithuanian text, in Gothic letters, is often uneven and not clearly printed. When out of one type, the printer simply replaced it with another! Between 200 and 300 copies were printed. Two copies remain today, one in the library of Vilnius University and the other in the library of Torun University, Poland.

During the next two centuries, more religious texts in the local language appeared as more people learned to read. This laid the foundation for Lithuania's literary language.

Several Lithuanian writers wrote patriotic ballads and prose during the 18th century Russian occupation. In 1864 the Russians banned the printing of the Lithuanian works. Despite the ban, poetic literature flourished. The poet Maironis was a leader in glorifying all things Lithuanian. His verses are still read and his poems have been translated into English. Prose writing developed after the ban was lifted in 1904.

Independence in 1918 ushered in a new era of creativity. Vincas Mykolaitis-Putinas wrote *Altoriu Sesely*, one of Lithuania's major novels. Women writers, such as Sofija Ciurlioniene and the poet Salomeja Neris, flourished.

Although some good pieces of prose and poetry were produced during the Soviet era, the repression stifled literary development overall. Today's writings reflect the writers' experience of the Soviet occupation, and many carry a dark, cynical, and sad tone. Popular writers today include Juozas Aputis, Vytautas Bubnys, and Vytautas Martinkus. The novels of Bubnys and Martinkus show the continuing attraction of folk themes. Emerging literature will certainly be influenced by the increased access to literature from other countries.

The Lithuanian Chronicles, *written in Old Church Slavic in the 1400s, relate Lithuanian legends, such as the founding of Vilnius, and stories of heroes and heroines.*

FROM BIRUTE MOUNTAIN

"Rolling wind-driven breakers ashore from the West,
Splash my breast with the chill of your waves, or to me
Grant your power, with such strength my spirit invest
That I speak just as grandly as you, Baltic Sea!

How I longed for you, infinite one! How I yearned
Just to hear your mysterious voice again!
You alone can appreciate me, you who scorned
Through the ages your towering waves to restrain!

Are you sad? So am I! And I do not know why;
It's my wish that the storm should howl louder for me:
Though it offers no tranquil forgetfulness, I
Always strive to be closer to you, Baltic Sea!

And I wish for a friend who will help me to face
All the storms of my heart and will soothe my heart's pain,
Who shall not by a dark look my secret betray
But restless as I am, shall ever remain."
                    —Maironis (1895), translated by Lionginas Pazusis

The architecture of Trakai castle mixes early Gothic style with local touches.

ARCHITECTURE

Lithuania's rural architecture arose from the people's farming background. Timber is by far the most common building material. The earliest houses had thatched roofs; later, wood shingles, clay, and tin were used. Some buildings have ornately carved woodwork. The skills of building are passed along from generation to generation with few changes being made along the way. The oldest wooden houses date back to the 18th century.

City architecture—fortifications and churches—was of stone, and it is these buildings that give the old cities their atmosphere today. Other buildings were made of wood until the 19th century.

Architectural styles followed those of western Europe. Early Gothic structures in Lithuania were heavy, massive buildings with thick walls, small windows, and massive buttresses. Typical examples of early Gothic architecture in Lithuania are St. Michael's Church in Vilnius, built at the end of the 14th century, and St. Michael's Church in Kaunas. Late Gothic churches of the 15th and 16th centuries are much larger and lighter structures. The best example of this is St. Anne's Church in Vilnius.

The High Baroque period produced the Church of Saints Peter and Paul in Vilnius and the church and convent of the Sisters of St. Casimir at Pazaislis near Kaunas. The convent is hexagonal and had a great copper roof. Over the centuries it has suffered from invading armies.

In the late 18th century, Classicism and Romanticism became predominant. Towns followed a rectangular grid. During the 19th century many of the cities' wooden buildings were replaced with stone structures.

After independence in 1918, an intensive growth of towns began. The countryside changed radically as the land was divided into individual holdings spreading all over the country. Rural architecture maintained the traditions of Lithuanian folk architecture.

Architecture took a step backward during the Soviet era. Huge, drab, cheap high-rises and complexes were the buildings of the day. Many are already dilapidated.

St. Anne's Church in Vilnius is built of special bricks of different shapes that create sophisticated ornamentation.

LEISURE

WINTERS ARE LONG AND COLD, and summers are very short in Lithuania. During the winter months, indoor activities are popular, especially storytelling by grandparents. Woodcarving and handicrafts created from flax and fibers are old traditions for occupying the short winter days.

During the summer, Lithuanians make the most of the warm weather. Forests, rivers, and lakes are within easy reach of city and country alike. In June, when the school term ends, many children are sent to stay with relatives in the country for the entire three-month vacation. Their mothers may accompany them, and fathers visit on the weekend.

In the country there is less leisure time than in the city. Leisure time is generally used for handicrafts. Women and girls' hobbies include drawing, knitting, crocheting, and sash-weaving. These skills are passed from mother to daughter. There are also get-togethers for name days and other church and traditional feasts, weddings, christenings, funerals, and even the slaughter of an animal, when neighbors and relatives are invited for a feast.

Young people from the country go to nearby towns to see plays, visit discotheques, or play sports. The most popular sport in Lithuania is basketball. In bad weather, young city people gather in cafés to talk, listen to music, and drink coffee. Most cafés also serve alcohol. A popular café among young people in Vilnius is Do-Re-Mi, which shows music videos and MTV in its bars. Vilnius specializes in beer bars, which are often cavernous cellars.

Opposite: **Enjoying a swim in a lake near Ignalina.**

Below: **Lithuanians like to relax in the country.**

95

TENDING THE GARDEN

Lithuanians like growing things—vegetables in their backyards, and flowers and herbs in their balconies and windows. Lithuanians are never more than a few generations from their farmer roots and almost all maintain some kind of tie to the land. Most urban people own garden plots on the outskirts of the cities and towns. In recent years, restrictions limiting buildings on these garden plots have become unenforceable, and summer houses have become more and more substantial. In the spring, summer, and early fall, families or groups of friends go there on weekends to tend the garden and fruit trees or just to relax. Older people who no longer have to worry about jobs just move out to the garden plot for the summer.

SINGING

Singing is a way of life in Lithuania. Family get-togethers are an occasion to sit and sing songs of their ancient land, mythology, customs, and folklore. Lithuanians are good at improvization. They have many lullabies, and even in lullabies, improvization is practiced.

People young and old join song and dance groups, traditional country bands, or pop groups to occupy their leisure hours. Some of the songs are about the sun, moon, and stars, and songs about magical transformations abound. In the songs about orphans, the moon is often asked to replace the father and the sun to replace the mother. A dead father sometimes reappears transformed into an oak. Other songs are about Lithuanian history and social protest. There are songs for dances and games, humorous and satirical songs, and songs about family life.

MOVIES

A popular way of spending an evening is to watch a movie at the local movie theater. Every town in Lithuania has a theater and there are more than 25 in Vilnius. Most of the movies are dubbed in Russian with Lithuanian subtitles. The major US and European productions eventually come to Lithuania, and there is also a small local movie industry.

Choral singing is a very popular activity. Most towns have a choir, many of them of professional standard.

Rollerblading is a recent addition to the sporting scene. This ramp is in Vilnius.

SPORTS

The most popular individual sports are non-competitive. Swimming is extremely popular, especially in rivers and lakes.

Fishing is a favorite pastime, and there are abundant fish in the thousands of lakes and rivers of Lithuania. Hang gliding is popular in the town of Prienai, where gliders are produced.

Ice skating and skiing have long been popular among young Lithuanians. Ice skating has declined to a certain degree, as fewer skating rinks are made in winter (winters are getting warmer).

Competitive sports are basketball, volleyball, and football. Of the three, the most popular is basketball, and every Lithuanian boy's hero is the player Sabonis.

DARIUS

The game at which Lithuanians excel is basketball. During the Soviet era, Lithuania provided the best players for the Soviet team, and in 1992 the national team won a bronze medal at the Barcelona Olympics.

The history of basketball in Lithuania begins with one of the country's great heroes, Steponas Darius. He was born in 1896. In 1907 his family emigrated to the United States, where he excelled at baseball, football, and basketball. He fought in France during World War I and returned to the United States with two decorations.

In 1920 he was one of the US volunteers who took part in the liberation of occupied Lithuania. He stayed in Lithuania for seven years. During this time he introduced basketball to the country and became a champion sportsman.

After his return to the United States in 1927, he worked in civil aviation and founded a Lithuanian flying club, Vytis. Five year later, he and his colleague, Stasys Girenas, set out to bring fame and glory to their newly independent nation by embarking on an epic flight from New York to Lithuania. They scraped together enough money to buy an old plane, which they called the *Lituanica.*

The plane left New York on July 15, 1933 and flew across the Atlantic in 37 hours 11 minutes, but it never arrived in Lithuania. No one knows why, but the plane crashed in Germany. Rumors that the plane had been deliberately brought down by the Germans did not improve international relations. The bodies were brought to Kaunas, then the provisional capital, and 60,000 people attended their funeral.

Despite its tragic end, many felt that the flight had put Lithuania on the map. The duo's portraits appeared on postage stamps, and 300 streets, 18 bridges, and eight schools were named after them. One of the most popular monuments to the heroes is near Anyksciai on a huge boulder called Puntukas. This is one of the country's mythical stones and is an ancient landmark. In 1943 a Lithuanian sculptor was in the country hiding from the Germans and he made a shelter beside the boulder. To while away the time, he carved a relief of the faces of the two pilots into the stone, adding the text of their will which had been written before they embarked on their historic flight.

TOURING

Hikers of all ages travel throughout Lithuania, visiting historical and religious sites. Battle sites are particularly popular. At these areas, people often stop to learn folk and patriotic songs.

During the summer, Lithuanians travel over their picturesque country by bike, foot, and car, and on the waterways by canoe, raft, and boat. Along the way, they visit history and craft museums, towns, cities, settlements and farmsteads, ancient places of worship, forests, hills, and lakes. Huge boulders are another attraction. One boulder is 75 feet (23 m) long, 21 feet (6.5 m) wide, and 13 feet (4 m) high.

Hikers rest and enjoy a stunning view.

SAUNAS AND ICE BATHS

Enjoying saunas is a popular leisure activity. Lithuanians love the alternate hot and cold that the sauna and their country's climate provide. Saunas are built near streams or lakes, so that after a session in the sauna, one can plunge into the icy waters of the stream or lake next to it.

In the wintertime, quite a number of Lithuanians take a dip in an "ice-hole." A recent fad is to swim in the Baltic Sea among the ice floes.

The town of Druskininkai, on the Nemunas River, is famous for its mineral springs and therapeutic mud, well-equipped sanatorium, comfortable holiday homes, parks, beautiful surroundings, and pleasant climate. This health resort, situated 87 miles (140 km) from Vilnius, attracts around 100,000 visitors a year.

Fishing through holes in the ice on a frozen lake near Siauliai.

Dancing in traditional dress.

DANCING AND GAMES

For Lithuanians, ballroom dances are more popular than games. Ballroom dancing became popular at the beginning of the 20th century. The Austrian waltz, Hungarian Vengerka, Spanish Padespan, Polish Krakowiak, and Russian Kokietka are danced on estates and in cities. The French square dance and the Bohemian polka are very popular in the villages. The Lithuanian quadrilles, the *sustas* ("SHOOS-tahs"), *jonkelis* ("YONG-kay-lis"), and *zekelis* (ZHAY-kay-lis") developed under Swedish influence.

In 1911, Matas Grigonis published a collection of 200 games. Formerly games did not differ from simple folk dances—both games and dances are based on singing and dancing. Games have retained singing throughout the years, whereas dances became more complicated and lively, until eventually instrumental music replaced singing.

Walking in a single or double circle, a half circle, or in rows is characteristic of games. The movements follow the rhythm of the song, becoming slower or faster along with the song. Movements consist of clapping, turning, bending, and passing through. In games, there is no limit to the number of participants. These types of games are rather old-fashioned now, and today they are most often played as demonstrations of a lost art.

CLAY WHISTLES AND BIRDHOUSES

Clay whistles are popular, and adults make them for their children in an astonishing array of shapes and forms. Lithuanian children are particularly fond of clay whistles made in the shapes of horses, riders, and lambs (for the boys), and ducklings, birds, and flowers (for the girls).

In the springtime, young and old alike busy themselves making birdhouses. These are mounted on poles near homes for the returning summer visitors—jackdaws, starlings, and others. Old wagon wheels are put on the roofs or on tall trees for the returning storks.

EASY PICKINGS

Lithuanians are fond of picking mushrooms in the forest, where there are over 100 varieties of edible mushrooms. People also go out during the summer and fall to pick wild strawberries, blueberries, raspberries, lingonberries, and cranberries.

Children make their own whistles from willow bark. Most young boys in Lithuania can make and play small *birbynes* ("beer-BEE-nus"), or reed-pipes, and *lamzdelis* (lum-zhe-DAY-lis"), similar to a recorder made out of wood or thick bark.

FESTIVALS

THE SPIRIT OF LITHUANIAN FESTIVALS has been kept alive over the years by strong family ties and the commitment of country people to their traditions. Lithuanian festivals are fostered by the many ethnic cultural centers, clubs, folklore ensembles, and places of worship.

Today, there are religious festivals, seasonal festivals, and ethnic festivals celebrated all over Lithuania. Sometimes elements of the two mix.

There are about 500 youth and adult folklore groups in Lithuania. Another 2,000 or so ensembles are active in secondary schools. Vilnius has some 25 folklore groups of university students, some of whom are very active in performing at Lithuania's festivals.

Opposite: **Preparing for a country festival.**

LITHUANIAN HOLIDAYS

January 1*	New Year
January 6	Three Kings' Day
January 13	Commemorates those who were killed or wounded by Soviet troops on January 13, 1991
February 16*	Independence Day (1918)
March 4	St. Casimir's Day—celebrates the coming of spring
March 11	Restoration of Lithuania's independence in 1990
March/April*	Easter
July 6*	Statehood Day—coronation of Mindaugas in 1253
August 23	Black Ribbon Day—signing of a secret pact between Hitler and Stalin to divide up the Baltic states (1939)
September 8	Nation Day. Birth of the Virgin Mary and the coronation of Vytautas the Great in 1430
November 1*	All Saints' Day
November 23	Lithuanian Soldiers' Day
December 25–26*	Christmas and Boxing Day

* *Official public holidays*

The pre-Christian festivals are based on the cycle of the seasons and crops. These people are celebrating the festival of the spring equinox on March 21, when day and night are exactly the same length.

MIDSUMMER DAY

St. John the Baptist's Day falls on June 24, which is Midsummer Day in the pre-Christian tradition. When Catholicism was brought to Lithuania, the Church incorporated this major holiday into the Christian activities by combining it with the saint's day, but the ancient traditions still predominate.

Most of the festivities take place on the eve of the holiday. Girls and women gather flowers and herbs, which are believed to heal illnesses if gathered at this time. The flowers and herbs are woven into wreaths and either worn on the head or floated down streams and rivers. People light bonfires and sing and dance around them, jump over them, and play games. The light from the bonfires can be seen from afar, shedding light on crops, thus ensuring protection from harm. The fires are believed to have cleansing and healing powers. Weeds from the fields are pulled up and thrown into the bonfire. Ashes from the bonfires are spread on the fields. At home the hearth fire is extinguished and then rekindled with a flame from the bonfire.

HARVEST FESTIVALS

Ancient Lithuanians' celebrations fell on the most significant days of the year: the solstices, equinoxes, and harvests. Since Lithuania is primarily an agricultural nation, it is not surprising that many festivals are connected with farming and animal husbandry.

There are many traditional festivities connected with the rye harvest. When the rye harvest begins, the first plants gathered are tied into a small sheaf. This bundle is called the Diedas (old man) or the Guest, and is set up behind the table in the place of honor. It stands there as a symbol of plenty.

Celebrating the rye festival in traditional style.

Before the main harvest, the family gathers with neighboring families at the far end of their rye fields to divide a loaf of rye bread. As they eat it, they say, "Bread meets bread."

The reapers leave a small bunch of rye stalks growing on the field at the end of the harvest. When they have finished, they stand in a circle around this bunch, cover their hands with scarves or aprons, and uproot the weeds from the bunch of rye stalks. These stalks are then braided and bent towards the farmstead to ensure that wealth flows from the fields to the household.

The reapers weave a harvest wreath from the best ears of rye for the head harvester to carry to the owner of the farm. The entire group of harvesters greets the landowner. The landowner then serves a big harvest feast.

Zemaitija, in the western part of the country, is famous for its Uzgavenes masquerades.

SHROVETIDE

Shrovetide, or Uzgavenes ("OO-zhe-GAH-veh-nes"), is celebrated in March on Shrove Tuesday, the last day before the 40-day fast for Lent that is traditional for Catholics. The verb *uzgaveti* ("OO-zhe-GAH-veh-tee") means "to eat well and heartily." This festival is full of humor, jokes, superstitions, fortune-telling, and feasting to celebrate the end of winter. It is a merry carnival, a masquerade full of pranks, with a drama performed outdoors to see off winter and welcome spring.

At dusk, men dress up in costumes with humorous, satirical, or animal masks. Some dress as evil spirits or demons with pitchforks. They go from house to house, deriding housewives or workers lagging behind in their chores. Many people dress up as traditional characters. Popular characters are Kanapinis, the Hemp Man, because during Lent hemp oil is used; a thief looking for something to steal; the pretending beggar; or characters rarely seen in the village, the doctor and the soldier. Animal figures include

108

horses, goats, and storks. Men disguise themselves as women and vice versa. An old woman, More—a symbol of the clash between winter and spring—is wheeled about in a cart. In one hand she holds a flail and in the other a broom, for she cannot make up her mind whether she should continue to flail last year's harvest or start sweeping the yard and doing the spring cleaning!

PALM SUNDAY AND EASTER

It is traditional to attend church on Palm Sunday morning with a bunch of juniper or pussy willow branches. Early on Palm Sunday, family members compete to get up as early as possible, so that the early ones can flog the sleepers with the green branches, singing: "It is not me who is flogging you, it is the Palm Sunday juniper doing it. Easter comes in a week. Do you promise me an Easter egg?" After the church service, the flogging continues in the streets. This is a way of wishing each other to be as healthy as the green twigs.

Bunches of dried grasses and flowers and small branches are sold on the street and near churches on Palm Sunday.

On Easter morning, the floggers receive Easter eggs. Easter eggs are decorated with wax designs then dipped in paint, or first given a color bath and then carved with a sharp knife or a piece of glass. Eggs are eaten on Easter morning. Children receive presents of Easter eggs from the Easter Granny, who leaves eggs in a neat nest outside the house or in a basket hanging from a tree. The children never see her, for she comes before sunrise in a little cart pulled by a wax horse (the wax horse would melt if she came after sunrise).

STORK DAY

The stork is central to many Lithuanian beliefs. It is thought to bring luck to homes. On Stork Day, March 25, farmers stir their planting seeds to increase the seeds' germinating power. It is said that snakes come out of their holes on this day. People avoid cutting wood or breaking off a branch, so as not to bring the snake home.

A Christmas Eve tradition is to be nice to everyone, pay all debts, go to the church for confession, and not visit neighbors without a good reason.

CHRISTMAS

Lithuanians celebrate Christmas Eve, or Kucios ("KOO-chi-ohs"), devotedly. The women scrub and decorate the house. In rural areas, the men clean the yard and prepare special fodder for the animals. When the day's work is over, everyone bathes and dresses in their best clothes. When the evening star appears, they sit down at the table. It is important to be at home for the Christmas Eve dinner, and sometimes people undertake long journeys to be with their family. Travelers are also welcomed.

For the evening meal the table is spread with hay in memory of the birth of Christ in the manger, and covered with a white linen cloth. Plates are decorated with a fir twig or myrtle. Sometimes hay is placed under or on each plate. A Christmas Eve wafer is placed on each plate. These wafers, *kaledaiciai* ("kah-le-DY-chi-eye") are made of unleavened wheaten dough, and hallowed in the church. A cross is placed at the center of the table. People sit down at the table in order of seniority, leaving empty spaces for absent members.

The meal begins with a prayer and the breaking of wafers. The head of the family breaks a wafer and shares it with all, extending greetings and good wishes. Everyone then does the same.

As a rule, 12 courses are placed on the table, one for every month of the year, so that the family will have enough food all year. The dishes are prepared from wheat, oat, and barley flour, groats, fish, mushrooms, poppy seeds, fruits, berries, honey, and hemp oil. No milk or meat is served. The meal ends with a prayer and the singing of a Christmas hymn. After the feast, both adults and children enjoy telling fortunes by drawing stalks of hay from under the tablecloth. On farms the hay from the table is then given to the animals.

The Christmas tree tradition came to Lithuania at the beginning of the 20th century. In 1908, pine trees were decorated on some farms in Zemaitija for the children of the laborers. In 1910 they appeared in a few schools and orphanages. After World War I, the custom spread to the cities, but not to the villages. The trees are decorated with patterns made out of straw, painted egg shells, and figures made out of pastry. These could be birds, horses, squirrels, lambs, moons, suns, stars, flowers, or other figurines.

Adults and children participate in a parade on January 6, which is known as Three Kings' Day.

ALL SAINTS' DAY

All Saints' Day, celebrated on November 1 and 2, is an occasion to remember the dead. On this day Lithuanians decorate graves with flowers, plants, and burning candles. It is thought that doing this brings the spirits nearer and helps to form a bond between the living and the dead. Since ancient times, Lithuanians have believed that after death, the soul separates from the body and continues existing among the living. In some places, bread is baked and distributed to the poor. This ensures that the coming year's honey and rye harvests will be plentiful.

FOLK MUSIC FESTIVALS

The best folk music performers are concentrated in Vilnius. Among the many folk music festivals held there, "Skamba, skamba kankliai" ("skahm-ba, skahm-ba kan-kli-eye"), held in the last week of May, is the most popular.

The largest folk singing festival is the Baltica Festival, held in a different Baltic city every year. The festival brings together singers and spectators from the three Baltic states and sometimes from Scandinavia as well. It was at the Baltica Festival in 1987 that the flags of Lithuania, Latvia, and Estonia were displayed together for the first time since Soviet occupation.

Lithuanians can now celebrate important days related to their history as a grand duchy and as an independent nation. Here people in traditional dress march in Vilnius to commemorate the Soviet invasion of Lithuania in June 1940.

ISLAMIC FESTIVALS

The Tatars celebrate two important festivals of their religion.

Aidul-Fitr is celebrated after one month of fasting between sunrise and sunset. The date varies, as the Islamic calendar moves back 11 days each year in relation to the Gregorian calendar used in the West. Houses are thoroughly cleaned, and new clothes are made and worn to morning prayers in the mosque. Then families come together to eat, exchange good wishes and presents, and to ask for forgiveness for any misunderstanding during the past 12 months.

Aidul-Adha is the feast of Abraham. It commemorates Abraham being asked to sacrifice his son. Animal sacrifices are offered and the meat is distributed to friends, relatives, and the poor. A special prayer is said in the mosques early in the morning.

Tatars dress up in new clothes for the Aidul-Fitr celebration.

113

FOOD

LITHUANIAN CUISINE, mainly based on potatoes, is rich and somewhat fatty. It is straightforward fare not far removed from the country, but it is not as plain as the food of Latvia and Estonia. The influence of the Tatars, Russians, Belorussians, and Poles is evident in the use of mild spices. Typical spices are caraway, garlic, onion, parsley, parsnip, dill, coriander, celery root, mustard, horseradish, fennel, and lovage.

Dishes vary in Lithuania according to the season. Animals are usually slaughtered in the fall and winter, so more meat is eaten at those times. During spring and summer, people eat more milk, vegetables, berries, mushrooms, and flour-based dishes. Fish is caught in the rivers, lakes, and sea. The country's natural resources are well used, and there has always been an abundant supply of good food.

Opposite: **Winter provisions are stored in the cellar, an important part of every house.**

Left: **Buying fresh strawberries in Vilnius.**

Loaves of dark rye bread for sale. The strong, sweet-sour taste of rye bread is ideally suited to the local beer, bland cheeses, and pungent cured meat and fish.

RYE BREAD

Lithuanians are very fond of dark bread made from dark rye flour, and they eat it at every meal. White bread is baked only on special occasions.

If the bread is baked at home, the loaves are put on cabbage leaves or calamus leaves when baking, which gives a special fragrance to the bread.

Bakers bake large oblong loaves, covered with maple, cabbage, or sweet-flag leaves to add flavor. The sign of the cross is made over the first loaf, and the sign of the cross is pressed onto the last.

Baking days are considered to be a special occasion during which homes are quiet and no one argues for fear that the bread won't rise. When visitors arrive on baking day, they have to wait until the bread is done so they can take one with them.

There are many superstitions associated with bread. A loaf of bread is inserted into the foundations of a new house to ensure that the family never runs out of bread. Farmers always plough a piece of bread into the first furrow in spring. The farmer's wife places a piece of bread under the first sheaf of rye during harvest time. When moving into a new house, a loaf of bread is carried into the house along with pictures of saints. A loaf of bread covered with a towel is always placed in a special place in the house. Newlyweds are greeted with loaves of bread at the threshold of homes. A bride always takes a loaf of bread and some leaven (yeast or fermented dough) from her mother's mixture to her husband's home. Important visitors are greeted with a loaf of bread on a towel. Slicing bread is always the duty of the head of the family.

MILK AND CHEESE

The dairy industry is very important in the Baltic states. Both fresh and sour milk is used in Lithuania. Milk is drunk sweet or curdled. Butter and fresh cheese are part of the everyday diet. Lithuanians make lots of soft and hard cheeses and a kind of cottage cheese called sweet cheese. This is made by boiling milk mixed with sugar and eggs, then adding a little curd into the boiling milk, thereby curdling all the milk. The curds are strained and caraway seeds are sometimes added for flavor. The mixture is then pressed into cheese.

During the honey harvest season, cheese is served with honey. Serving cheese with honey is considered a very special treat.

Cheese is served with coffee on special occasions and at festive events. A special, dense, yellow cheese is made for the Midsummer festival. Cheese is always served with buttered bread. It is also given as a present when visiting friends and relatives.

ZEPPELINS

3 lbs (1.35 kg) raw potatoes
1 lb (0.45 kg) cooked potatoes
l lb (0.45 kg) minced beef or pork
1 onion
salt and pepper to taste

Grate the raw potatoes and squeeze out all liquid through a cloth. Peel the cooked potatoes, then mash them and mix with the raw grated potatoes. Add salt and knead to mix. Put aside.

Chop the onion and fry until brown in a little oil. Add the minced meat and the salt and pepper to the onions. Mix well and sauté until slightly brown. Reserve some of this mixture to use as a topping.

Take a piece of the potato mixture the size of an egg and flatten it out in the palm of the hand. Place a heaped tablespoon of the meat stuffing in the middle of the mixture. Cover the meat stuffing with the edges of the potato mixture so that the meat is sealed in it. Place the Zeppelins in salted boiling water and cook for 25 to 30 minutes. Remove the dumplings from the water and put them on a heated serving dish. Pour the sautéed meat and onion mixture on top and serve.

THE MANY USES OF POTATO

Potatoes were brought to Lithuania in the 18th century and very soon became the most popular item on the Lithuanian plate. Lithuanians love boiled potatoes served with sour or fresh milk.

Potatoes are used in soups, dumplings, porridge, pancakes, and puddings. Grated potatoes are used to make sausages. A typical Lithuanian dish is boiled potatoes served with pounded and fried hemp seeds.

Each housewife has her favorite recipe for the potato. Potato pie is served with sour milk, cottage cheese, sour cream, and fried cubed bacon. Since the turn of this century, zeppelins—potato dumplings stuffed with meat and onion— have become a favorite Lithuanian dish.

OTHER DISHES

The Lithuanian diet has become fairly uniform throughout the country, although certain slight differences remain between different regions. Zemaitians are still fond of all kinds of porridge and *kastinis* ("KAH-sti-nis"), a kind of butter. Dzukians specialize in buckwheat and mushroom dishes. Suvalkians love *skilandis* ("ski-LAHN-dis"), smoked pig's stomach or bladder filled with minced meat and seasoned with pepper, garlic, and sweet cottage cheese. Aukstaitians love to eat large pancakes for breakfast.

Meat comes mostly from cattle, sheep, goats, and pigs, and less from fowl. Pork is the most common meat in the Lithuanian diet. Lean pork and bacon is boiled or baked. Meat is salted or smoked for longer storage. Freshwater fish is an important food source for those residing near rivers and lakes. Smoked eel is a special treat among the people of the Baltic coast. Eels are found in Kursiu Marios and some rivers and lakes, and they grow to be 4 feet (1.2 m) long and up to 9 pounds (4.1 kg) in weight.

Beets, cabbages, and turnips have long been a part of Lithuanian cuisine. Beet greens and roots are eaten freshly boiled or pickled, or used in soups. Cold beet soup, with sour milk, cucumbers, dill, and eggs is a popular dish in the hot summer months. Fresh or pickled cabbage soup is a common dish. Some 20 species of mushroom are eaten in Lithuania. They are used to flavor soups, especially beet soup, during Lent. A cream soup with vegetables, such as potatoes, peas, carrots, or cabbage, with pieces of flour dough or pasta is frequently eaten for dinner.

Fruit and vegetables can be bought fresh from the markets.

Milk is an important part of the Lithuanian diet, as a drink, in cooking, and in other dairy products.

DRINKS

Milk is the most commonly consumed beverage. Coffee is the most popular hot drink, with tea a distant second. Both coffee and tea are served without milk.

The most popular alcoholic drink is beer. Lithuanians started brewing beer in the 16th century. Today there are nine commercial breweries, and bottled beer is common and of high quality.

Homemade beer is still brewed in some districts. The head of the household begins a special meal by pouring a mug of beer from a pitcher and saying to the guests, "To your health. Drink, brothers, and celebrate!" He then spills a few drops, drinks the cup dry, fills it again and hands it to a guest. The gathered people reply, "Be healthy" and "To your health." In this fashion, the cup makes it way down the table.

Sweet commercial soft drinks are widely available. The most popular is Fanta. One kind of soft drink cordial, called *salde* ("SAHL-day"), is made from plain or germinated rye. Birch sap flavored with blackcurrant leaves is popular as a drink.

Midus ("MI-doos"), or mead, is an ancient weak alcoholic drink made from honey. It is produced commercially today, although the original recipe has been lost. Lithuania also produces several types of liqueurs as well as vodka and champagne.

AT THE TABLE

Lithuanian dining customs are rigidly structured and strictly observed. Each family member has an assigned place at the table. The head of the household sits at the end by the wall in the place of honor. Traditionally, men sit on one side of the table with the women opposite them. Guests, travelers, or even beggars who arrive are always invited to the table. Important guests are seated in the place of honor or beside it.

Meals always begin with the slicing of bread by the head of the household, who then passes it around. Slices of bread are always broken with two hands because producing the bread require two hands. Lithuanians pride themselves on their hospitality and will relentlessly urge visitors to eat a little more. No one, even guests, rises from the table until everyone has finished eating.

KITCHENS

In old country houses, wood stoves are still used (with a gas or electric stove as a standby). Fuel is the dry branches and chopped wood of fallen trees collected from the forest. The stoves also keep the houses warm.

Houses always include a cellar, even in high-rise buildings in cities. In the countryside, cellars are dug outside and covered with an earth mound. Winter provisions are kept in the cellars: potatoes, beets, carrots, cabbages, onions, pumpkins, squashes, apples, sauerkraut, pickled cucumbers, and dried mushrooms. Most housewives preserve fruit and berries picked from the garden or forest.

In Lithuanian kitchens, a clay pot is used as a double boiler for soups and zeppelins, and a potato grater (electric or hand-turned) is indispensable because meals made out of grated potato are an everyday affair.

After the winter season, when the first summer meal is served, whoever remembers first that it is the first meal of the summer will unexpectedly strike the person sitting next to him or her on the head with a spoon saying "Here's something new!" The struck person can take no offense and can retaliate only against someone younger.

LITHUANIA

LATVIA

Baltic
Sea

Mazeikiai
Joniskis
Birzai
Venta
Musa
Musa
Rakiskis
Palanga
Telsiai
Siauliai
ZEMAITIJA
Seduva
Panevezys
Klaipeda
Minija
CENTRAL LOWLANDS
Anyksciai
AUKSTAITIJA
Nerija
Raseiniai
Jura
Kedainiai
Kursiu
Taurage
Nemunas
Dubysa
Ignalina

Kursiu
Marios

RUSSIAN FEDERATION

Sakiai
Nemunas
Jonava
Neris
Kaunas
Kauno Marios

Sesupe
Prienai
Birstonas
Trakai
VILNIUS
Vilnia
Viliya

SUVALKIJA
Nemunas
DZUKIJA
Juozapines
(963 ft / 294 m)

POLAND

- ● Capital city
- ● Major town
- ▲ Mountain peak

Feet	Meters
16,500	5,000
9,900	3,000
6,600	2,000
3,300	1,000
1,650	500
660	200
0	0

Druskininkai

BELARUS

| 0 | 10 | 20 | 30 | 40 | 50 Miles |
| 0 | 20 | 40 | 60 | 80 Kilometers |

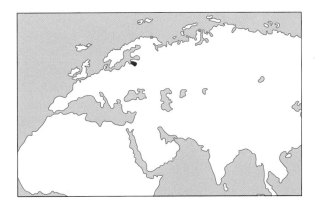

QUICK NOTES

OFFICIAL NAME
Republic of Lithuania

LAND AREA
25,174 square miles (65,201 square km)

POPULATION
3.8 million

CAPITAL
Vilnius

LONGEST RIVER
Nemunas (582 miles / 937 km)

HIGHEST POINT
Juozapines (963 feet / 294 m)

LIFE EXPECTANCY
Males: 63 years; females: 75 years

PRINCIPAL LANGUAGE
Lithuanian

MAJOR RELIGION
Christianity (Roman Catholicism)

NATIONAL FLOWER
Rue

NATIONAL BIRD
Stork

NATIONAL ANTHEM
Lietuva, tevyne musu (Lithuania, Our Fatherland)

CURRENCY
Litas. US$1 = 4 litas

IMPORTANT DATES
February 16 – Independence Day (independence in 1918)
July 6 – Statehood Day (coronation of Mindaugas in 1253)

MAIN EXPORTS
Electricity, light industrial products, food products

MAIN IMPORTS
Petroleum and natural gas, machinery, chemicals, light industrial products

HISTORICAL FIGURES
Mindaugas, united tribes into one Grand Duchy
Gediminas, extended Lithuania's territory
Jogaila, grand duke who became King of Poland
Vytautas the Great, grand duke at the height of the Grand Duchy
Antanas Smetona, first president after independence in 1918

LEADERS IN POLITICS
Vytautas Landsbergis, leader of Lithuania after the first democratic elections in 1990
Kazimiera Prunskiene, first prime minister
Algirdas Brazauskas, elected president in the first direct presidential election in 1993

LEADERS IN THE ARTS
M. K. Ciurlionis, painter and composer who is the founder of modern Lithuanian culture
Petras Kalpokas, early 20th century painter
Maironis, patriotic lyric poet
Velio Tormis, choral composer
Osvaldas Balakauskas, modernist composer
Salomeja Neris, poet
Vincas Mykolaitis-Putinas, poet and novelist

GLOSSARY

animism
The belief that all things have a spirit.

atheism
The belief that there is no god.

birbynes ("beer-BEE-nus")
A reed whistle.

delmonas ("dayl-MOH-nus")
A traditional decorative handbag.

glasnost ("GLAZ-nost")
Openness; a Soviet reform policy of the 1980s.

jonkelis ("YONG-kay-lis")
A Lithuanian dance.

kaledaiciai ("kah-le-DY-chi-eye")
Christmas Eve wafers.

kankles ("KAHN-klis")
A traditional stringed musical instrument.

kastinis ("KAH-sti-nis")
A kind of butter popular in Zemaitija.

klumpes ("KLOOM-pus")
Traditional wooden shoes.

Kucios ("KOO-chi-ohs")
Christmas Eve.

lamzdelis ("lum-zhe-DAY-lis")
A wooden recorder.

midus ("MI-doos")
Mead, an alcoholic drink made of honey.

patarle ("PAH-tehr-lay")
A proverb.

perestroika ("peh-reh-STROY-ka")
Restructuring; a Soviet reform policy of the 1980s.

polytheism
The worshiping of many gods.

raudos ("RAO-dohs")
Laments or farewell songs.

Sajudis ("SAH-yoo-dis")
A political organization that advocated Lithuanian independence.

salde ("SAHL-day")
A soft drink cordial made from rye.

Seimas ("SAY-i-mahs")
The Lithuanian parliament.

skilandis ("ski-LAHN-dis")
A dish of smoked pig's stomach or bladder filled with seasoned meat.

sustas ("SHOOS-tahs")
A Lithuanian dance.

Uzgavenes ("OO-zhe-GAH-veh-nes")
Shrovetide festival.

vytis ("VEE-tis")
The charging white knight on a white horse that is the state emblem of Lithuania.

zekelis ("ZHAY-kay-lis")
A Lithuanian dance.

zeppelin
A potato dumpling filled with meat and onions.

BIBLIOGRAPHY

Avizienis, Raza, and William Hough. *Guide to Lithuania.* Connecticut: The Globe Pequot Press, 1995.

Chicoine, Stephen, and Brent K. Ashabranner. *Lithuania: The Nation that Would be Free.* New York: Cobblehill, 1995.

Flint, David C. *The Baltic States.* Connecticut: The Millbrook Press, 1992.

Geography Department, Lerner Publications. *Lithuania (Then and Now).* Minneapolis: Lerner Publications, 1992.

Harbor, Bernard. *The Breakup of the Soviet Union.* East Sussex: Wayland, 1992.

Insight Guides: Baltic States. Hong Kong: APA Publications, 1994.

INDEX

INDEX

INDEX